CW00747254

REAL HOMES

REAL HOMES

INSPIRATION BEYOND STYLE

Solvi dos Santos

Text by Phyllis Richardson

Thames & Hudson

Page 1 A converted warehouse in Mallorca has been turned into a modern home furnished in a careful mix of periods and styles.

Previous pages Real homes are all about mixing styles and objects, as in a kitchen arrangement, left, that evokes simple country comfort; the contemporary portrait against the rough-finished stucco wall signals the owners' more sophisticated tastes. In contrast, a clean-lined room with modern furniture, right, becomes a backdrop for a varied collection of curious items.

This page The antique statue accented with a fluorescent hoop perfectly sums up the relaxed attitude to art in this Upstate New York house.

Opposite A deeper tone on a wide, open wall space feels both grand and personalized.

CONTENTS

The appeal in all of these displays is in the unabashed celebration of each chosen item, whether the plaster dogs' heads (modelled on the family pets) in a house outside Amsterdam, crockery and objects in a Tuscan farmhouse, assorted collectibles in the house of an American antiques dealer or proliferating stacks of books in a Mallorcan palace. Objects of personal value take pride of place.

INTRODUCTION

What is a 'real home' in the twenty-first century? Of course there are a multitude of homes around the world that are real, lived-in places. But if we're still interested in style, in some kind of comfort, taste, sophistication, but without the stamp of anonymity impressed by a hired interior designer, where do we begin to create a home that is also personal and a joy to inhabit? The answer, as photographer Solvi dos Santos has discovered in visiting each of the rooms featured in these pages, is to look at the homes of creative people today and find inspiration there. What she has found, in Africa, Asia, America and Europe, is that a new way of thinking has emerged that in some respects is a return to old values and a reverence for tradition but also a more open attitude towards including different styles or influences in a coherent but highly original interior.

The idea is not to present trends or models that are set up for imitation, but to reveal how people in the age of financial meltdown, environmental awareness, political upheaval and rapid technological acceleration make a home that satisfies fundamental requirements but also becomes a private work of beauty and self-expression. Bearing in mind that the prevailing attitude is one of a certain amount of style, the range for expression is wide. Indeed, the point of this book is to demonstrate a broader vision of the artful home interior, one that reflects a rejection of the consumer-led, fashion-

Carefully drawn contrasts can paradoxically feel like a natural coming together of styles. Modern hues paired with more traditional elements or ornate, period furnishings create arrangements that have an easy elegance.

conscious approach, in favour of the personal, the individual, the thoughtful, the provocative or the endearing.

Looking back over the last few decades, the aspirations of creative people now seem to recall something of the counter-cultural feeling of the 1960s and 1970s, whereby the younger generation were eager to overthrow their parents' lifestyle choices and values. Today, the difference is that the culture that people want to do away with more and more is the overly mechanized production pieces and the showroom interiors that have filled so many pages of so many interiors magazines. It's a return to basics, for lack of a better term, where 'basic' means something that has intrinsic appeal, either by being an expression of genuine craft or by having a particular resonance for the owner, whether it is an ethnic carving chosen during time abroad, a work of art or a select heirloom. Here, the overturn of previous habits is about hanging onto things rather than throwing them out. In fact, much of what appears in the book is demonstrably against the 'throw-away' culture that grew up in the last century around the idea that a degree of style could be achieved by using cheaper goods that were only intended to last for a short period, say while children were young, and then be replaced at a later time by something more expensive, and presumably more permanent. But people weren't only throwing out cheaply made manufactured goods. The showroom interiors are often the result of a complete design overhaul that did away with anything that didn't fit, whether a bespoke design or a flea-market find, and left little of sentimental value or personal attachment, at least in the public realms of the house. Here, you won't see rooms that have been stripped out and re-designed in perfect colour-matched harmony, but rather rooms that feature objects and art that are meaningful in some way to the people who own and display them and have been added to other objects of different styles or provenance but which for some reason have been kept and cared for.

This is not to say that there is not a strong element of design in what follows. On the contrary, it is design that works a bit harder and more creatively. Rather than offering a totally honed

suite of furnishings that are all matched to the wallpaper, the draperies and each other, these are arrangements that make use of new and old, vintage and modern, inexpensive and dear, and still manage to get along wonderfully. The result is that every arrangement is unique, not something that will have been reproduced from a manufacturer's catalogue, because it comes from a very personal collection and sense of style.

If each room is so personal, one might ask why it is worth showing them at all, since every one of us has our own personal taste. But like someone who dresses with originality and flair, though not necessarily in designer garments, these are rooms that demonstrate a particularly inspiring visual appeal. They also evoke an enticing atmosphere and resonate with bold creative spirit. Most of the rooms shown here are about experimentation and a free choice of materials, colours, textures and objects. It is the surprising versatility, the pleasant variation that is like a well-orchestrated piece of music that makes a room hum with energy or seductive calm. These pages are also a testament to creativity and to devotion to the home as a place of personal pride, hospitality and sanctuary. These are rooms that are lived in by the people who have created them, people who are less concerned with making a design statement than with making connections through the things they have around them, and through those things to the people they invite to share their spaces.

This may seem a very commonsense approach, but we have in the West a long history of 'over-decoration' and imitation in our interiors. In the early sixteenth century, the noted Parisian society hostess and cultural patron Madame de Rambouillet caused a sensation when guests to her literary salons first beheld her newly decorated 'chambre bleue'. In this room, the painted woodwork, carpets and velvet hangings were matched in design and colour. Such was the impression of the interior that the French Queen, Marie de Médicis, who was renovating her apartments at the Palais du Luxembourg, sent her decorating team over to investigate the 'chambre bleue' and bring back ideas. And others soon began to copy the wholly integrated style. The North Drawing Room at

Antique and modern join gracefully when colours are subdued and each piece of furniture or object has space to breathe. Traditional furnishings have contemporary appeal against a spare background; iconic modern furnishings cohabit with treasured antiques.

Formal arrangements are not always stuffy or uninviting. These grand Nordic rooms show respect for their own distinguished long heritage but are softened by a simple overall style.

Ham House was given over to a similarly dominant colour scheme in the 1630s, but in white and gold.

Of course, only the very rich could afford such decorative overhauls, but the habits of the upper classes were adopted by others depending on their means. Decorative 'schemes' became very popular in the eighteenth and nineteenth centuries when people could use pattern books to order furnishings and decide on decorative details according to certain styles. But there were objectors. In the late nineteenth century in Britain John Ruskin railed against decoration without integrity, saying, 'Better the rudest work that tells a story or records a fact, than the richest without meaning.' The poet and craftsman William Morris concurred, 'Have nothing in your houses that you do not know to be useful, or believe to be beautiful.' In the USA, the novelist Edith Wharton, in *The Decoration of Houses*, argued against the jumbled interiors of the Victorians, in favour of a more serene, classical sense of balance and harmony. Though she too suggested patterns and styles to follow if in doubt.

In the twentieth century the rise of glossy interiors magazines made us all voyeurs of other people's houses, usually the most elegant interiors, and we absorbed this perfectly arranged and skilfully photographed 'eye candy' through their pages and, however unconsciously, aspired to it. But the turn of the new century, with all of the economic and social factors that have forced many of us to reconsider the luxury goods, temporary furnishings and the waste produced not only by cheap, short-term objects, but also by tossing out perfectly good pieces simply because they do not 'fit' a particular decorative code, has brought a change.

This book presents hundreds of interiors, organized room by room, that demonstrate the idea that while a room might be beautifully arranged, it need not eschew personal elements, treasured objects or quirky mementoes to do so. From practical elements such as stone floors and storage in the entrance hall, to the luxury of an ornate gilded eighteenth-century table used as a work desk, to the artful whimsy of books stacked in a mountainous but tidy pile against a living room wall, these pages reflect the variety and art of inspired everyday living.

Natural materials such as wood and stone have a universal appeal – the uneven tones and inherent irregularities keep any space from feeling overly formal or restrained. Unfinished wood is a useful option for both outdoor furnishings and indoors, where it can take on a sculptural presence.

Clean modern design doesn't have to be off-putting. This contemporary house has a grand architectural presence and a beautiful sea view but is full of works by local ceramists, painters and crafts people.

Outdoor rooms are part of the real home, with a feeling of stylish ease carried across from the interiors. A well-chosen position, with comfortable, robust furnishings and a few luxurious decorative details, offers a living space that flows naturally and invitingly into the open air.

The double-height, sky-lit entrance to this barn-style home makes a bright introduction to an art-filled contemporary living space. The dark stone floor, door and timber beams contrast with the white-painted wood-clad walls.

ENTRANCE

The entrance to a house tells a lot about how people want others to feel when coming into their home. There can be anything from a high sense of formality that warns you not to touch anything, to a casual disregard for first impressions. Here the idea is for an entrance to be an interesting introduction to a conversation, but one with a cultured friend who might set your mind working with bright new ideas.

The entrance is the part of the house that says 'welcome' and many other things to family, friends and guests. The initial impression given here sets the tone for the rest of the living spaces. The entrance can, of course, be a very utilitarian area where coats, hats, gloves, umbrellas, all of the outdoor accoutrements, are stored or cleverly displayed. The overall use and effect are determined somewhat by architecture, whether it's a modest-sized vestibule, a narrow hall, a stair landing or a wide open area flooded by natural light. The wonder of the spaces in these pages is the sense of good design, even if the household necessities are not hidden away, when boots, umbrellas or a well-travelled bicycle sit so naturally, not like pieces from a designer's box but as objects ready for use, only beautifully so.

In medieval European houses, the door led immediately to the great hall. In some parts of the world such as the Arabic countries and the Mediterranean, the entrance to a house is buffered by a courtyard, so that access to the private realm is further

removed from any walkway or road. You will also find this sort of approach in the more traditional buildings in the cities of France, Spain and Italy, where apartments are arranged around a courtyard, and the entire complex is reached via an imposing street door that gives no hint as to what lies behind it. This sort of delayed entry creates a procession of spaces, a growing sense of intimacy and calm as you travel from the busy public world to the private space indoors.

In other countries there may not be a courtyard but a front garden that offers another kind of 'prelude' to the entrance of the private house. Or it may be the house's entrance itself that lets you into the more private areas only by degrees, say where there is a grand, double-height stair hall that signals the house's overall proportions and emphasizes the fact that you are still in the more 'public' realm, not yet enjoying the private living spaces.

If you stop for a minute and think about what it is to stand on the outside of the house as a stranger or on the inside as a family member or guest, you begin to have a different idea of the impact of those

first moments inside the door. This is not a comment on the pressures of all-over design, but an observation about opportunities to enhance an often overlooked living space. Inside and outside are already worlds apart, but some people, as shown here, have made the most of the transition, laying out an entrance that presents an immediate welcome to their private realm of the home.

As the following pages demonstrate, even an entrance utility area can have wonderful appeal when given some creative thought. From an organized array of hooks and shelves for coats and hats, to the added character of vintage wooden boxes or oversized pots for storing umbrellas and boots, to making a display of some more colourful elements of outer wear, the very basic elements of storage and utility become rather lovely snapshots of daily life. The idea, after all, is not to deny that a house is lived in but to celebrate the style and tastes of those who do reside there and to use the spaces as well as possible.

It might seem a rather grandiose claim, but art can also be part of this 'first room' of the house or there can be more general expressions of colour and design, so that the entrance is not so much an initial encounter with impeccable tidiness as an introduction to the personal tastes and affections of the inhabitants. A large open entrance hall can act as a fitting stage for a large painting or sculpture that announces the creative tendencies of the residents, becoming an object of interest for guests and offering an enticing taste of a larger collection to be found and savoured inside. In one interior here it is a welcoming dog, not the real thing but a sculpted one, that greets visitors as they enter. The gesture is both artful and friendly, a particularly happy combination that helps to make guests feel at home.

There is some discussion about formal versus utilitarian entrances but in these pages both are approached with abundant charm and elegance. In some houses the entrance is a grand double-height hall, while in others it is a more enclosed space that might open to a corridor or stairs, bringing guests through the house by degrees. Here the light and colour can be used to draw visitors towards the interior. Strong colours in the entrance have a particular appeal.

Entrance halls that say 'well-groomed' but not impersonal. Objects such as the painted desk and chair, left, and the vintage travelling case, recycled painting frame and iron chandelier, opposite, make connections with the people who live in the home. These two houses may be miles apart in style, but the open spaces are equally inviting.

There will also be different ways of presenting the entrance to a house depending on whether it's in a rural or an urban context. In the countryside, where there is likely to be more open space around the house, and more room overall, there is a better chance of creating an imposing entrance in the form of a great hall. However, as the images here show, there are plenty of ways to create a striking entrance even with a modest utilitarian space. Natural light helps to make the entrance more welcoming, as does some attention to objects of art and colour. And then there is the question of flooring. In the room where people enter the house from the outdoors, or may go in and out repeatedly, it makes ample sense to use a robust material on the floor. This can be anything from hardy rustic wood planks to elegant but hardwearing mosaic tile, a pebble floor or great stone slabs. In an urban environment where space is tight, the entrance is more likely to be a vestibule but some people have worked a kind of magic in these tight spaces, making clever use of storage, sightlines and natural light.

In some places where cold or very inclement weather is common, the entrance will offer welcome shelter and protection from the chill and rain. Entering a house with a wood-burning stove on a wintry day may have become a cliché, but it's an experience people still respond to. However, in much warmer climates, it is the shadowy coolness that the first step into the house extends to the visitor, a soothing respite from harsh sunlight. This traditional approach is still favoured by some people in these regions, while others would rather celebrate the strong natural light with an expansive, cool white interior that spreads out in dramatic fashion from the first move inside.

So in these pages, the entrance is much more than a blank hall at the front door. It is an introduction full of light, colour, art or utility all animated with appealing personal touches. The objects, whether decorative, fanciful or practical, are arranged to provide a first glimpse of a real home that is lived in and appreciated by its occupants. It is a way of saying welcome to our private world and of sharing a bit of those things that give the house its own character and pride.

The entrance hall often doubles as a storage area, but it can still have a decorative style. Personal objects need not be discreetly hidden away, especially when there is such a collection of interesting items to display. Houses from South Africa to Umbria, and from Mallorca to Nantucket, demonstrate that the entrance can make an intriguing introduction.

Left Visitors to this cottage in New England are welcomed by a chequerboard-painted wooden floor and an open period dresser filled with vintage crockery.

Left A pair of antique dining chairs says 'welcome' in a centuries-old house in the Swedish countryside.

Above A painter's retreat in Provence keeps to simple furnishings from different periods against a homey rustic background.

Opposite The clean, Puritan style of this hall pervades the house of the painter Jamie Wyeth. Off the coast of Maine on the East Coast of America, the rugged landscape contrasts with the bright, trim interior.

Flooring in the entrance area signals how formal or immediate the transition indoors will be. Pebble and stone floors in the outer hall leave room for muddy shoes and boots. Mosaic tiles suggest a bit more refinement and a carpeted floor means you have officially arrived inside.

Art and objects in the entrance to the house suggest something of the personality, taste and creative interests of the people who live there, whether it's a piece of sculpture, ethnic art, a patterned rug or a designer chair.

A flat in Ibiza, opposite left, makes some quick cultural references in the hall. A house in Norway, left, and an apartment in Copenhagen, opposite below right, show off their artistic flair. This page, a flat in a converted industrial building in Paris welcomes guests with singular pieces of design.

Opposite and below An architect-designed chalet in Turkey features old wood flooring imported from the USA. Oversized pendant lamps add to an industrial chic styling. The house's large open spaces are sparsely decorated with a few elements to suggest its use as a mountain ski lodge.

Above right Despite its New England location, this house on Martha's Vineyard keeps to a clean contemporary approach.

Right The house of English ceramic artist Rupert Spira in Somerset retains much of its rustic farmhouse appeal with his larger works providing moments of elegance.

Left This house in the Mallorcan countryside was restored and renovated by the owner, architect Antonio Obrador, and his wife. The couple allowed the period features to stand and used traditional textiles to soften the stone surfaces.

Opposite Another resident with a fondness for local textiles is the dealer and collector who owns this house in Cape Town. The bold geometry of the native cloths gives them a contemporary edge that suits the owner's creative approach.

Colour is often used as a guiding principle in decoration but when it already exists, from a former period, it adds a layer of history and life. With minimal restoration, antique painted effects become glorious fragments of another age.

Opposite A seaside house on the south coast of Sweden offers a cool, breezy welcome.

Right On an island in Estonia, summer houses are dotted through the forest. This spare interior suggests an unfussy, relaxing retreat.

Above A house in southern Norway maintains the traditional painted plank walls.

Right Dutch residents in Menorca have restored this old traditional house to a place of modern comfort with an unconventional ambience.

Far right A summer house on the coast of Maine greets visitors with a household pet in carved wood.

Warmth is one of the most important aspects of the home. Wood fires will always draw people in and provide a feeling of comfort and security. A traditional stove in any culture has the same appeal.

An apartment in Ibiza mixes the high windows and folding shutters of an older period with classic modern furnishings.

LIVING

There are a range of labels in the English language – sitting room, parlour, lounge, reception room, drawing room – that describe the space that we now designate for 'living'. It seems a pretty arbitrary description; of course we live throughout the house. This is the room without a specific function, unlike the kitchen, dining room, bedroom or bathroom. It is the room or area where we relax, watch television, read, entertain and gather as a family. So the requirements, or the ingredients, can be rather numerous. It's a room that should offer some comfortable seating, it should offer warmth, in the form of a fireplace or some variation on a hearth. The living room is also a place to display some of the things that we enjoy having and looking at, collections of art and objects that reveal our private tastes but which we want to share with guests.

By the eighteenth century the house in Europe had evolved from a place of work and shelter to a refuge for privacy and comfort. Rooms became divided according to function so that later a living area, rather than the kitchen or bedroom antechamber, became a place to receive guests. Furnishings became not just utilitarian pieces but objects that conveyed a certain style or taste. Western cultures began to produce more varieties of chairs and sofas, while in Eastern and Mediterranean homes, sitting on the floor, albeit on a brightly woven rug and amidst soft cushions, was more common.

In the twentieth century some designers developed models for increasingly ergonomic furnishings, while others explored more inventive shapes with less regard for comfort. But in most places these experiments were conducted in what we call the living room.

If the entrance offers guests a greeting, then the living room of a house is something like a warm embrace. This is the main room that attracted many an all-out design makeover in the recent past, and was used to show suites of fashionable furnishings in highly coordinated arrangements that were a tribute to their unique design pedigrees. While there is certainly nothing wrong with choosing high-design pieces for a living

townhouses, from apartments in antiquated city centres to new-build mountain lodges in the Scandinavian wilderness. And all are places one can imagine living in because, although they express a truly remarkable sense of style, they also radiate a feeling of warmth, comfort and personal attachment.

There are several factors that help determine how approachable a living space feels, such as how spare or plentiful the interior. A very sparse, minimal scheme might appear too clinical but an interior that is too full can create an unpleasant visual chaos. Order and balance are good things, but they can be achieved using a variety of styles and elements. In these pages we find that living

Rooms for living are often all about peace, relaxation and the personal, a particularly luxurious combination in any interior. A mood of calm elegance can be achieved in a variety of architectural settings – from classical style to modern to clean-lined contemporary.

room, this is the place where a house can really show its own personality. The textures, colours, patterns and objects can create a strong visual connection while arrangements of furnishings can be physically welcoming (or off-putting). The trend towards the over-designed living room had a real limiting effect on the all-purpose character of this space, which in the pages of some glossy interior magazines sometimes had the feel of a stage set. What is interesting to see in these pages is how even minimalist devotees have created living rooms that still feel approachable, with furnishings that are not forbidding but actually invite use. Too often, a meticulously designed living space has evoked the comment that though it was beautiful one 'couldn't imagine living there', or that the rooms feel somehow impersonal, and so have more of the ambience of a hotel, perhaps a beautiful luxury hotel, but a public rather than private space, nonetheless. That sentiment is very much against the grain of this book.

In this chapter, the houses range from centuries-old farmhouses to high-style, architect-designed city

spaces are vibrant, well-orchestrated and stylish, but they are also full of singular objects and furnishings that provide a real sense of individual character.

It makes for an engaging atmosphere, for example, when there is an object or work of art to provide a focus for a room, and it is more calming when there are some areas that are more restrained and leave space for a kind of visual pause. Textures can make a room inviting as layers of fabrics, even in neutral tones, add a sense of depth to the living environment. Of course, it is helpful if there is some kind of control over a palette of materials, so that each can be appreciated and understood. But, again, the idea is to start with the elements that have personal appeal and then arrange them into a coherent scheme.

The living room must be versatile, as we have mentioned, having to accommodate everything from day-to-day family activity to possibly more formal entertaining. And there are wide-ranging options in terms of spatial arrangements that sometimes do not occur to even the most avid reader of interiors magazines. This is because

The varied arrangements and design motifs of rooms from Connecticut and Nantucket in the USA, to France, Estonia and South Africa share a combination of style and comfort. A warm dose of natural light, some inviting soft furnishings, and a collection of interesting art and objects are key ingredients to all of these appealing living spaces.

there are times when a house is adapted from a non-domestic structure and the living space has to be articulated within an existing open-plan area. These spaces (as shown in the following chapter) can offer a relaxed flow of light, air and movement, but must also be in tune with the rest of the house. Even an older domestic building might require you to rethink accepted notions of how living space is set out and dressed up. An enclosed living space might suggest a greater sense of formality, but it can also create a lovely sense of intimacy. In the houses photographed here, some people have differentiated between a living room for relaxed family use and a more formal sitting room that is reserved for use apart from children, being designated for guests, while others have combined all uses into one room, including extensive collections of art, books and objects that demonstrate the strong personal connection between the house and its owners.

Strict adherence to tones and schemes can impose a sense of formality on a room and the people in it. Relaxing against a grandiose design background tends to make one feel hedonistic or louche rather than naturally at ease. But to repose in an interior that has more individual personality is like being in the company of an inspiring friend.

And while a well-furnished room with a cosy fire might seem like the ultimate achievement in comfort, houses in warmer climates with more open arrangements that play to the indoor–outdoor lifestyle are redolent with a sense of holiday ease even with a permanent, year-round habitation. A living room that is awash in natural light, with large doors opening to a terrace and a view of water, and where a sea breeze can flow freely throughout is an altogether different experience from a wood-panelled room lit with an open fire or a high-rise apartment overlooking a spray of city lights. But the examples chosen here confirm that all of these spaces can be wonderfully appealing, and not just because they are in grand houses with luxurious furnishings and amenities, but because they each represent such individual character and choice of elements mixed with a strong aptitude for style. The individuality even affects the degree to which

A white-painted background makes even a room full of varied furnishings feel like an exercise in cool simplicity, and is a fitting setting for modern design.

Above A cool modern house in South Africa designed with ample built-in shelving for displaying pieces from the owner's collection, such as these examples of ancient pottery.

Opposite The white-washed walls and tile floor of this Ibiza apartment in a well-preserved period building make a cool backdrop for the resident's collection of vintage objects and furnishings.

an older house might be restored or left in a more rusticated state. In some of the living spaces here, the residents have taken very deliberate decisions about how much is renewed, particularly in some older houses in Spain, Morocco and Italy, and how much existing architecture, however ancient, is allowed to make its presence known in the interior.

Other people whose homes appear here have embraced fully modern treatments in new, architect-designed buildings with living spaces that are more spare, even minimalistic, compared to their historic counterparts. In these rooms, too, style and personal details help to make living spaces that are not only beautiful, but are also somewhere an outsider could actually imagine living in, and would like to live in, even if the architecture, modern or traditional, is not to their particular taste. This idea is well illustrated by some of the interiors from the grand Scandinavian or French country houses that are kept in their original style but with various esoteric touches that give them individual personality and flair and keep them from appearing as museum set-pieces.

In Ibiza, a spare, modern living space is filled with bright rugs, large plants and vivid artworks. In Oslo, a house of classic modernist design invites visitors to enjoy its iconic but well-loved contemporary furnishings and a towering collection of books. In a cool white villa in Indonesia, white-washed walls and traditional timber elements mix with simple furnishings. In Spain, Italy, Norway, Turkey and the South of France, rooms full of antiques, all personally chosen and functional, make heritage part of an everyday living experience, rather than something precious and out of reach. In these rooms, decorators, artists, designers and architects have poured into their living spaces the things that inspire them and make them feel at home. Whether they have the atmosphere of a private library or an open-air pavilion, are part of a grand historic house or a clean-lined contemporary villa, these are rooms where people come together to relax in the company of friends and family or just to enjoy the environment they've created for themselves. And it's easy to see how one might live there.

Iconic modern furniture establishes a sense of history and architectural aesthetic. The clean lines and innovative forms look fresh even today. They remind us that great style has great longevity.

Left Classic designs, such as the Mies van der Rohe 'Barcelona' day-bed, help maintain the modernist aesthetic in a house near Oslo. It was designed by Norway's most avant-garde architect of the 1930s, Arne Korsmo.

Below A pair of 1960s Ross Littell 'Luar' chairs make a nice period vignette in this Scandinavian retreat.

Opposite This home was also designed in the 1930s by the Norwegian modernist Arne Korsmo. It is a fitting backdrop for a collection of mid-century and earlier designs such as the 'Grand Confort' chairs by Le Corbusier and Charlotte Perriand. The tall space benefits from the large vertical window, which provides plenty of warm daylight.

Left A converted warehouse in New York, the home of Dutch artist Gerd Verschoor, is enhanced by modern furniture and his own works, including the circular paintings.

Below left Cool and white, this Parisian flat is home to a gallery owner and collector of works by young, emerging artists.

Below right An art collector in Germany has created a modernized interior inside a traditional-style building for his collection of contemporary art, which includes a painting by Jean Zuber and sculpture by Axel Cassel.

Opposite A farmhouse in Ibiza has been modernized and the interior kept to a minimal palette by architect Pascal Cheikh Djavadi and interior designer Victor Esposito. Cheikh Djavadi also designed the sofa and day-bed, while the headlamp sculpture is by the Afghan artist Mahmoud Akram.

Artworks displayed in the public living spaces are more than just a statement of sophistication, they impart the collecting passions and talents of the owners, and infuse the whole atmosphere with a tangible creative vibe.

Left This newly built house in Norway has a minimal scheme that allows the artworks to take precedence.

Left A former designer has filled her architect-designed villa with pieces of art and unique furnishings, including this chair by Norwegian designer Terje Ekström.

Opposite right In this light-filled living room, a pared-down, bright white background is given depth and a richer ambience by some colourful elements of art and furnishings. The carpet was made to match the triptych painting. The abundant natural sunlight pouring in through the floor-to-ceiling windows warms the room and allows the large potted plants to flourish, echoing the luxuriant greenery outside.

Right A South African fashion designer with a penchant for colour has made her home a gallery for the work of a favourite local painter Karel Nel.

Below right Near Cape Town in South Africa, a modern house designed by Stefan Antoni has a wall lined in corrugated metal, making references to poorer housing nearby. The contrasting styles set up a dynamic space for modern art and design.

Ethnic and tribal art have a particular effect on an interior, especially when the rooms are otherwise spare, allowing each piece to make a genuine impression.

Opposite The home of a French designer in Indonesia is a cool, clean setting for his collection of large timber and palm elements, as well as smaller traditional crafts.

Above Glass pieces designed by Benny Motzfeldt are displayed in the Paris apartment of a Norwegian designer.

Above right A converted barn in Provence has become home to a finely curated collection of rustic art and furnishings.

Right Carved African artifacts are exhibited in the home of a Norwegian collector in Ibiza.

Displaying treasured art and objects, memorabilia and collectibles was once thought detrimental to design purists but these personal expressions can all be part of a thoughtful, welcoming and even stylish living space.

Opposite From the quirky to the truly creative, these little displays demonstrate that an object doesn't have to be high art to be inspiring.

Above This apartment in a centuries-old building in Ibiza wears its age openly but has a clean, modern atmosphere that leaves plenty of room for the range of antique, vintage and ethnic pieces favoured by the resident.

Right This living room is located under the roofline of an antique structure where open skylights illuminate the white-washed spaces and the collection of unusual art and furnishings.

Minimal is a word that has fallen in and out of fashion and back again. These rooms show how the clean lines and sharp planes of the modernist-style house can take on a much more lived-in atmosphere through natural lighting, well-placed furnishings and bold works of art.

Left The levels in this new modern-design house in Spain are used to articulate rooms within a large, open-plan ground-floor interior. Polished concrete makes a cool, sophisticated setting for choice ethnic objects and furnishings.

Opposite A modern mountain retreat in Scandinavia eschews the ski-lodge cliché for cool, rectilinear forms and giant proportions. Concrete and steel are softened by the warm wood floor, generous natural light and upholstered seating.

Neutral backgrounds are calming and warm, but they can also show texture, layers and creativity.

Opposite above A small house for a young couple with children features an unusual built-in shelf system for displaying books and objects. The over-stuffed sofas and animal-skin pattern rug offer a soft contrast to the sharp angles of the shelving.

Opposite below left Rustic mixes with classical in a converted barn.

Opposite below right Pale tones, a rusticated antique armoire and an upright canoe used as a bookcase create a friendly atmosphere in this Nantucket home in the USA.

Above and right The Icelandic home of textile artist Erma Steina, who specializes in weaving natural materials and even paper fibres to create lampshades and large screens, as well as floor coverings, has a gentle modern ambience. She painted the moveable panels.

The fireplace as the centre of the house is not just a nod to nostalgia. It draws attention to a communal area, offering comfort and a pleasing idea of home.

The home of antiques dealers in Spain, opposite, shows a nice mix of rustic and modern elements. While the white soft furnishings in this room in Maine, above, contrast with the dark wood. In South Africa, above right, and Tuscany, right, the beams and woodwork are like antique objects on display.

A manor house in southern Sweden, this page, and an old home in Normandy both share a pleasant ambience of faded grandeur.

Above A portrait of the actor Marlon Brando presides over the living area of a house set on a hilltop near Cannes in France.

Left Intriguing finds from the local antiques shops fill an aged manor house owned by a Norwegian artist living in western France.

Opposite The flagstone floor, arched doorways and rough ceiling show the house is from a different age, but the bold wall colours keep the rooms feeling bright and interesting.

Rich period rooms with traditional seating can easily feel outmoded and uncomfortable, but with some modern interventions in terms of colour and furnishings they can become dynamic spaces that feel much more livable and inviting.

Opposite above Comfortable elegance in the home of embroidery artist Edith Mézard.

Opposite below left Classical, antique and eclectic mix together in the house of an architect and collector.

Opposite below right A stately home in Finland exhibits a taste for neoclassical refinement.

Right On the outskirts of Istanbul this period house is layered with history and fascinating decorative detail, from the marble-covered pilasters to the patterned overmantel and wall and ceiling painting.

Traditional furniture and objects still have a place in stylish, contemporary rooms, even when mixed with pieces from other periods.

Left The home of architect Hans Parr Lampe in Oslo is filled with a combination of furnishings from different periods and places but set out in a well-orchestrated arrangement.

Above A deep leather armchair and club-style sofa gathered around a wall of sketches and portraits has the warmth and focus of a gentlemen's library.

Left A fondness for African textiles and contrasting furnishings such as the Regency-style sleigh bed yielded this lively but tasteful interior.

Mixing not only periods and styles, but also patterns, colours, textures and shapes, materials and provenance can produce rooms with intriguing layers and variation.

Left Rich ochre-coloured walls recall vernacular building types in this South African home where a designer/collector has displayed natural wood pieces, a tiger-patterned chaise longue and a chandelier of ostrich eggs with vintage chairs and table.

Above and right More artful combinations of colour and pattern.

Colour and texture on walls and flooring can make rustic interiors feel modern and lively, suited to plain furnishings, but also contrasting touches of Baroque ornament.

Left A Menorcan interior wears its rustic charm proudly, with vivid blue walls and a traditional hanging lamp lighting a small day-bed covered in colourful textiles, all tucked into a comfortable corner.

Below Paler shades in walls and furniture denote a more open, public room of this Menorcan house. The open beams painted in the same light hue as the walls and ceiling make the room feel more expansive.

Opposite and right A summer island house speaks of easy living with bare plank flooring, large windows and simple furnishings. The blue-painted walls recall a bright summer sky.

Left This old, traditional-style wooden house on a fjord in Norway maintains its historic character with the stove against the red walls.

Cosy is a word that many designers try to avoid but it is an effect that most people relish in areas of their own homes. Although in some cultures we might call it something else, the idea has become an integral part of traditional design.

Above and left The painted pine walls of these mountain retreats create a snug-feeling interior. The carved wooden day-beds and cushions covered in pieces from traditional Norwegian national costumes reflect the local heritage.

Opposite The snug Scandinavian feeling has been translated to this Vermont retreat, designed by architect Ross Anderson, who believes in small houses set in large untouched landscapes. The cushioned window seat is a perfect reading spot on a wintry afternoon.

Relaxing moments are to be had in rooms where colour, style and atmosphere are calm, where natural light is soft and the overall feeling is welcoming.

Opposite In Ibiza the traditional built-in sofa structures are covered with thick cushions. Rusticated walls contribute to the relaxed style.

Above and left Striped ticking fabric creates a simple, inviting mood, both in a French retreat and an old Swedish farm.

Artifacts and pieces of traditional craft give a room a sense of history and tradition, while also providing wonderful

moments of colour, texture and pattern.

Right A house designed by the Egyptian architect Hassan Fathy, in close collaboration with artists Yannick Vu and Ben Jakober, features fretwork windows, intricately laid mosaic tiles and richly patterned textiles inspired by traditional Moorish design.

Below References to North African style, combined with spare, modern architecture.

Opposite A beautifully restored Moroccan *riad* in Marrakech features ornate, textured wall panels, complex decorative mosaics and richly carved woodwork, while a day-bed and cushions add comfort.

Cultural traditions in architecture and design, whether part of an original building or as inspiration in a new space, have an almost spiritual effect on the life of a house.

Sunlight in a white room has many dimensions as surfaces and textures absorb and reflect the natural glow.

White-painted interiors are warmed through with natural light that feels luxurious against comfortable furnishings. A converted rural outbuilding, opposite, which retains its utilitarian heritage, has become a place for peaceful repose.

Opposite The ultimate in simplicity: a striped hammock beckons in Formentera.

Above right The house that architect Jørn Utzon built for himself in Mallorca uses blocks of sandstone to blend with the cliffs.

Right A summer house on a Nordic island. The pastel décor ensures there is little distinction between outside and inside.

A designer who set up house in a huge old mill in La Rochelle, France, kept the rustic character of the place very firmly intact, while adding personal artistic flourishes like the shell-encrusted cloth screen to the right.

OPEN PLAN

Open-plan living dates back to medieval halls that weren't built with partitions and where everyone slept on the floor as close to the hearth as rank would allow. The division of domestic houses into rooms that could be closed off and heated was a great improvement on the quality of life. In the 1960s, however, there was a vogue for open-plan living areas that reflected a more casual lifestyle influenced by the architecture of modernism, houses designed in the International Style and by adherents of the Bauhaus such Mies van der Rohe, whose Tugendhat house (1930) in Brno, the Czech Republic, became an icon of sophisticated modern living. The living area was separated only by a gold-and-white onyx partition and shared a large window wall that allowed the extensive open interior space to bathe in warm natural light. The dining area was semi-enclosed by a curving section of naturally grained Macassar ebony. Like many open-plan interiors after it, the living spaces were kept feeling warm and interesting by the use of such rich materials.

But this style of open-plan modernism was never widely available to the public at large. The materials and methods remained rarified examples of a lifestyle only achievable by those with access to sophisticated architects and designers. Still the well-designed open-plan house with large sections of glass is perceived as an elite brand of housing. However, advances in technology, in the quality and efficiency of glass, and in heating, such as under-floor methods, have meant that it is easier and more comfortable to live in an open-plan arrangement than in the past.

But an open-plan space does not always mean a clean, modern space. Some of the houses here are definitely of the minimal and modern school, but others are more rustic, like the new Norwegian house where the open-plan ground floor revolves around a dramatic slate hearth and brick fireplace. Its interior comes alive with a large collection of art. Other examples show a twist here and there that bespeaks the individual personality of the owner and the contemporary context, without appearing unachievable to those with lots of creative enthusiasm.

While some people prefer defined series of rooms or feel that open-plan living is only for the warm climate of the tropics, others find great potential in the free flow of space. In some rooms here the residents have made use of the generous space to exhibit large works of art, as in a substantial modern house in Ibiza, where the white-washed walls and stone floors are a natural setting for oversized sculptural Indonesian wooden artifacts. Others have found a place for oversized pieces of furniture that would otherwise be hard to fit into an interior scheme.

Of course, most people do not live in a space that is completely without any designations or limits. Different functions are distinguished by furniture groupings, by the placement of rugs or changes in flooring materials. The room, instead of being designed for a single function, becomes a composition of sorts. In some of the more open spaces shown here, it is a change in pattern or colour that indicates the different areas of the open interior. A large bookcase, a richly patterned textile, even a curtain attached to a timber beam can be used as an effective spatial divider while also adding some colour, texture and pattern. In other rooms, the furnishings might be carefully grouped, with, for example, the sofas and armchairs gathered around the hearth, a dining table set out separately on a woven rug or just positioned at a different angle to create a distinct area. Then there might even be a desk or a singular seating area beneath a window off to one side.

Unusual spaces can be created by layering levels within a double-height room and leaving the internal volume open plan so that different parts of the structure are visible and the whole feels light and accessible.

One of the most appealing aspects of these interiors is, indeed, the very 'open' effect – that freedom of movement and activity that is possible in this kind of space. It feels generous, luxurious, even if the overall square footage is smaller than that of a standard house. The living 'space' has an airy atmosphere, although anchored by cosy furnishings. The dining area has an expansive feel, making it easy and natural to move from the table with your after-dinner drink or coffee to the armchair near the fire.

The open-plan designs of the modernist era were usually of the low-slung, single-storey typology. But here many of the open-plan spaces are also double-height rooms that are full of natural light entering from windows at ground level and from openings much higher up. There are light industrial buildings, the classic artist's loft which became an inexpensive way of finding living space in the 1950s and 1960s, but a very sought-after sort of elevated bohemian trend in the 1980s and 1990s. In this chapter we show, for example, a wonderfully varied set of domestic spaces carved out of a former button factory in New York, where original elements such as cast-iron columns are joined by creative partitions and minimal use of striking modern furnishings.

Open-plan living spaces are found in a number of converted types of housing, whether former warehouses or factory premises, old stables or other agricultural outbuildings or even religious meeting houses converted for domestic use. These cathedral-style interiors can feel very grand, even if they are modestly decorated. In some cases, such as in a traditional house in Provence or a light industrial loft space in Marseilles, the open interior includes a mezzanine. While in others the ground floor remains open but bedrooms and bathrooms are placed on an upper floor, so the house has the best of both worlds, intimate private rooms and a luxurious open interior for relaxing and entertaining.

Traditional-style houses can also be arranged in open-plan style, with the original period features left in place and an open mezzanine used for a more intimate seating area or as a route to the private rooms in the house.

Many people worry about the potentially cavernous atmosphere of an undivided interior, especially in modern houses that lack the presence and character of large rustic timbers or other historic elements. But in these pages even more modern and minimal open spaces have a comfortable ambience owing to the use of large plants, sculpture, textiles and floor treatments, and generally a creative attitude to organizing and displaying art and objects.

In fact, it is now a popular trend to open up spaces previously divided into separate rooms, in order to achieve more expansive areas for each function without having to add on to the floorplan of the house and to allow for the flow of natural light and air. It is a brave step to start taking out walls (and not just because of structural questions), but the interiors here are all the product of people with determined creative and programmatic ideas who aren't afraid to use them.

Another concern with open-plan interiors is to do with the open kitchen area, and the lack of cover for cooking aromas and messes. There are more than a few clever ways that even a very open kitchen can be separated from the main living space, visually and spatially without walls. Perhaps the best aspect of choosing an open-plan arrangement is that it allows for numerous solutions. Rather than doing away with walls entirely, one might choose to add one or more, but site them differently, and have partitions instead of walls or, as we've seen, use furnishings, storage units, a hearth or a uniquely created screen in cloth, wood, glass or any manner of material to insert partial divisions while maintaining that free flow of space and light.

The open-plan style and the way it is used has evolved to a more common occurrence. For people who create their own style of interiors it has become a place to experiment with colour, texture and design but also to rethink traditional rooms and their uses. Like so many of the modernists' ideas, open plan is something that, with the advance of materials and technologies (such as heating systems), is experiencing a revival and, as these examples show, it is one we can celebrate.

Opposite A newly built house in Norway features an open, double-height living space with the brick fireplace and slate hearth in the centre of the room. The unfinished lodge-pole columns, naturally grained plank flooring and fragmented slate maintain the rustic atmosphere while the clean finishes and array of artwork reveal a more modern side to the home.

Above This classic Swedish country house was given a modern update by knocking through walls and opening the ground floor into a single, much brighter space.

Above right A small beach house in Mallorca features a low partition with Islamic patterned cut-outs.

Right An old farm building was given new life with a large open living/dining room. There is even room for a little work desk to the left.

Above left Located in a mountainous area of Europe, this house was built to integrate with its dramatic natural setting. The architects have differentiated spaces within the open-plan area by creating a series of open niches.

Left A loft space in a former industrial building in Marseilles, France, has become a factory of creative ideas under the influence of its artist owner.

Levels within a tall, open-plan space create a sense of interest and dynamism in an interior. The different functions of the house are all readable in the various access points, although there are still enclosed private spaces.

Above A new-build house on the west coast of Norway keeps to firm modernist lines. The white walls, orthogonal planes and chrome fittings are offset by warm tones.

Right On a beautiful site on the River Daugava in Latvia, this house, designed by Zaiga Gaile, shows how a modern, open interior can transform even an older building into a space of light and pleasing proportions.

Double-height rooms have an immediate feeling of luxury, allowing for more natural light and for the eye to travel freely without physical barriers.

A modern apartment on the top floor of a late nineteenth-century building features a six-metre-long (20-ft) table made from three mahogany logs set on steel trestles. The roofline and structural pillars have been integrated into the interior with one unifying colour.

The clean lines and sharp planes of the modernist-style house can take on a much more lived-in atmosphere through well-placed furnishings and vibrant works of art.

Above A new, modern Scandinavian house functions on three levels but keeps an open middle floor that helps free circulation in and around the stairway. The glass partition makes the open-tread stairs part of the transparent, light-filled main living area. A change in flooring material denotes the different functions of the space.

Left A modern villa in Oslo was given a bright renovation by opening up rooms into one long, light space. The kitchen and dining area are at the far end with the hearth marking the change to the living space. The home office, which necessitated an enclosed room, is through the door on the left.

Natural light is key to the ambience of any room, but is particularly important in a large, open-plan space where dark corners can be either welcoming or gloomy.

Above A late nineteenth-century house near Amsterdam was given a lift, quite literally, by architect Piet Hein Eek, who made the decision to raise the roof, introducing the clerestory above the wall on the right and another row of window panes to the main window wall.

Left This former farm outbuilding was given a new lease of life as a home. The low-roofed structure was brightened with a tall extension surrounded by ample glazing to keep the interiors warm and bright.

Opposite Purchased in New Jersey in the USA, this 1830s barn was transported in pieces to Martha's Vineyard where it has become home to a young couple. The open space reveals a fascinating network of old timber beams and struts; the rustic plank flooring has been retained. The wooden floor of the main living area has been painted to indicate a division of spaces.

Opposite The penthouse at the top of an office building in Oslo, Norway, has been kept open and free flowing on the main floor. An office, a jacuzzi and a roof terrace are sited on the mezzanine.

Right A former religious meeting house has been transformed by a young couple who wanted space and light to display their own designs, such as the rugs created by the owner for Ikea.

Below Opposite ends of a top-floor former industrial space turned family home. Keeping the space open allowed the A-line roof and timbers to be part of the interior scheme. The swing gives the children something to do on rainy days and makes good use of a conveniently located beam.

Opposite This white-painted modern house with a polished concrete floor is just right for the warm weather of Ibiza and makes a good backdrop for the owner's collection of oversized wooden pieces from Indonesia.

Below and right Created in a nineteenth-century button factory, this SoHo loft in New York has just the right mix of original elements and cool modern interventions. The block partitions organize the space, while a sparse array of artful furnishings gives attention to each piece.

Loft spaces appeared to have their heyday in the 1960s but there will always be a fashion for the wide open interior with oversized elements. Details of a previous industrial life only add to the romance.

An open-plan living area in a converted church builidng in the Hudson Valley of New York also includes an office and a dining area. The house is owned by Chris Lehrecke and his family. Lehrecke designs and builds furniture: the solid-wood table is his own design.

DINING

The Roman historian Suetonius wrote that the first-century Emperor Nero had a dining room, or *coenatio rotunda*, which was circular in shape and was made to rotate night and day in imitation of the motion of celestial bodies. It was part of his Domus Aurea, 'Golden House', the grandest palace Rome had ever seen. One façade was faced entirely in gold, while inside most of the walls were inlaid with mother-of-pearl, studded with gems or covered in frescoes painted by Nero's favoured decorator, Fabullus. But it was in the rotating dining room where some of the most hedonistic activities of the emperor and his friends took place, a sign, perhaps, of the connection between eating too well and behaving without moral compunction.

In 1784 Marie Antoinette had her small dining room at Versailles turned into a billiard room. The larger dining room was sufficient for the dozens of people who might dine at the palace on a given evening and she could easily accommodate her close friends in her own rooms. At this time it was still customary to move furnishings around, so a table for eating might be brought in or moved to the centre of the room and then stowed at the side when not in use. In the previous year, the profligate Prince of Wales, later George IV, visited Brighton for the first time and soon began having visions of the palace he might build there away from the prying eyes of court and the press. He wanted to be able to hold his extravagant parties and cavort

with his mistress without censure. He did so lavishly at Brighton Royal Pavilion, which was constructed in an Indian architectural style and completed by John Nash in 1822. The interiors were an exotic mix of Mughal, Islamic and Chinese styles. One of the grandest rooms of the palace was, and still is, the exuberant Banqueting Room, where the Prince Regent sometimes held 70-course dinners. Its walls and ceiling were completely covered in painted decoration of faux architectural detail and Chinese domestic scenes. The room was lit by dozens of candles and chandeliers, including the centrepiece which is nine metres (30 feet) high and weighs a ton.

There are examples too numerous to mention of grand historic houses sparing no expense in embellishment, and often it was the dining room that was given the most extravagant attention. In modern years, at the height of the popularity of designer-led interiors, the dining room was frequently a forbidding place of rigid formality. Even the most contemporary arrangements appeared untouched and untouchable. Looking at any of these set-pieces, where every platter and candlestick was part of a design 'scheme', it is hard to imagine sitting at the table, let alone eating there.

But if this book is about any one thing, it is about how real life meets good taste and creativity. In the dining space there are elements that just need to be there for practical reasons, and there is the awareness that family meals are not always, or often, beautifully orchestrated events. But it is also important to maintain a sense of ritual which has been a part of communal eating for centuries, bringing us together, as friends, family or invited guests. We want to be able to have a sense of occasion without a staid atmosphere, a feeling of enjoyment without fussiness, and, despite what Nero might have thought, an idea that such pleasures are not part of a grand indulgence but a small celebration of daily life.

For some of the spaces we've gathered here, 'dining room' seems a rather grand term, as rustic and rough-hewn as they present themselves. Others, such as those antique Scandinavian mansions, are more redolent of a fashionable evening. With

An assortment of dining chairs in a variety of styles helps to create a more relaxed atmosphere. Wooden chairs from different centuries keep company in mixed rustic or modern settings.

chandeliers, matched dining chairs and a linen table cloth, these spaces are certainly more formally arranged, but the difference between these and the set-pieces of the designer trademark era is that they leave room for quirks, for individual expression. This might be an odd candlestick, a chipped piece of vintage crockery, a bit of ethnic weaving or a chandelier that doesn't hang quite so perfectly and an impromptu bowl or vase of fresh flowers, the kind that look not like a professional arrangement, but some that might have just been brought in from the garden. These are trivial details, but a dining space that can be well dressed and accommodate the trivial and the personal is one that speaks of actual mealtimes rather than staged vignettes.

The dining spaces we've put together in this chapter range from the rustic to the antique

contrast help make all of the spaces more friendly and interesting places. Some rooms definitely begin with a traditional approach and then add modern elements such as a contemporary chandelier, or it might be a very rustic setting with plank flooring and unfinished timber which is set off with a velvet-upholstered Baroque chair and candlestick, or pieces of cutting-edge contemporary art. Other rustic dining areas, such as those in converted farm buildings, have had minimal restoration but have then been appointed with iconic pieces of mid-century design. In one instance, the dining space is tucked into a niche created by centuries-old stone walls, while in a crisp white modern villa in Ibiza, the rough cliff-face is an immediate presence just beyond the dining-room door.

The rugged strength of stone imparts a sense of elemental grandeur, a comforting sense of longevity, continuity and the solidity of tradition. Simple furnishings and warm natural light create a calm, livable atmosphere.

On a hilltop in Mallorca, a dining area set in an old building once used as an olive press. Some parts of the building date from the eleventh century, and the owners have spent more than 30 years restoring it. Eight-metre-high (26-ft) ceilings and windows set in the thick stone walls and the bare slab flooring recall the building's heritage.

and the cool modern. Some are small cabinet-style rooms such as the early eighteenth-century Norwegian chalet where the walls still bear their original decorative painting. Other 'dining areas' might just be a long table at one end of an open-plan room, as in the converted church set in the Hudson Valley of New York. There are urban apartments in Copenhagen, Paris and Tallinn, artists' studio tableaux and modern country eating spaces.

There are cosy, candlelit spaces and high-style formality, but with a twist. The spaces are elegant, relaxed, stylish, romantic, with approaches too varied and layered to specify by name. But some themes emerge such as the larger, farmhouse-style dining spaces that offer an essay in periods and styles of chairs. Some would call these mis-matched, others wonderfully charming. And then there are those with matched sets of vintage furnishings and accessories that are still quirky in their arrangements and context. Mixing and

Many of the dining spaces are open and bright, while others are unabashedly dark and moody, the candles and low-light chandelier providing soft illumination. In the less formal surroundings of real homes dining spaces are also storage and display spaces. So stacks of crockery are as artfully exhibited as hung porcelain plates, and parades of glassware, pots or soup tureens have an eccentric, casual and utilitarian appeal.

And just as the chairs don't need to be perfectly paired, the table doesn't have to be a standard purpose-built piece. There is a wonderful array of furniture that has been re-purposed or built as dining tables in this chapter. On the East Coast of America in a barn, which was taken down and reassembled in a different location, the owner had a table constructed to seat up to 35 people. It is accompanied by a fine set of unmatched antique and vintage chairs. In a house in Mallorca, the dining area is in the space once occupied by an old olive press, and large parts of the original mechanism are still intact. A house re-designed for a couple by Piet Hein Eek is a showcase for his trademark distressed and re-purposed wooden doors and panels which give the dining area and kitchen an older, more vintage atmosphere. There are large farmhouse tables, stylish modern tables, polished antique tables covered in white linen and others draped with a casual, coloured cloth. With the growing popular interest in home-cooking and gastronomy, the dining room is attracting new focus. The aim is not a feast of over-indulgence, stylistically or otherwise, but to bring people together in a comfortable, artful environment to share good food in good company and enjoy conversation as inspirational as the setting.

Wood in many forms is a material that most people respond to: whether rough and natural or highly polished and in colours that vary from pale blonde oak to the darkest ebony, it has universal appeal.

Opposite above Architect Gustav Langenskiold and his wife, Ylva, restored and renovated a house in Provence and it is now the place where they both live and work. The dining room's classic Arne Jacobsen 'Series 7' chairs are family heirlooms.

Opposite below Fitted with an assortment of simple, Shaker-style furniture, this house in Normandy belongs to Russian artist Yuri Kuper.

Below A still-life vignette in a Swedish country house.

Right A mid-twentieth-century house outside Amsterdam was re-designed by Piet Hein Eek, and features his trademark distressed wood and re-purposed panels for doors and cupboards.

Variations in texture, tone and colour in natural materials such as wood, stone and brick add layers of interest even to sparsely decorated rooms.

Opposite Now a house, this former stable on an island off the coast of Finland seems to reach back to Nordic mythology. The building has been kept in a very raw, elemental state, with original thick block granite walls and a timber ceiling.

This page A villa in Ibiza inspired by the iconic modernist Le Corbusier is integrated into the surrounding terrain, with the rocky cliff-face part of the room here and in other rooms. The minimal décor lets the natural setting take precedence.

Storage and display of crockery, utensils and cookware have been a part of kitchen and dining spaces for centuries, and the practice is gaining new popularity.

Opposite Part of a huge kitchen space in an old Swedish manor house, this eating area has been restored to Gustavian style but then finished with modern touches such as the 1958 Poul Henningsen PH5 pendant lamp for Louis Poulsen.

Above left This large dining space in the Nantucket summer house of interior designer Constanze von Unruh used to be a garage. The high, A-frame ceiling and ample natural light belie its previous utilitarian function.

Above right Once an 1830s carriage house, this building was converted into a home by architect Hugh Newell Jacobsen. Some of the original elements, such as the plank flooring, were retained, while modern furnishings were added.

Right The Paris apartment of artist and designer Christian Astuguevieille features his own-design rope-faced dresser, as well as the original stained-glass door from a previous century.

Above The interior walls of
this early eighteenth-century
Norwegian farm retain the original
decorative painting by Olav
Hansson. The house has been in
the same family for generations
and they have worked to maintain
its historic character.

Left The dining area of the La
Rochelle house of artist Blott Kerr-
Wilson features a bar covered in
her signature shellwork.

Below Dining spaces are also living spaces, as in this cabin on the beach near Cape Town in South Africa, where open plan means all-purpose. The door was taken from an old train car.

Right A simple dining space was added to the ground floor of a French manor house. It wears its heritage openly with old stone flag flooring and a rough stone basin. The terracotta colour helps warm the cool, shaded room.

Right The home of antiques' dealers in Ibiza features an antique wood- and coal-burning heater and nineteenth-century iron garden furniture.

White with plenty of natural light makes for a calm, relaxed atmosphere. Hard surfaces are rendered softer with lots of sunlight and a few personal objects on display.

Opposite A Scandinavian period house with traditional interior and original wallpaper and stove.

Above Constanze von Unruh's basement dining area gives the illusion of al fresco dining.

Right A simple space overlooking the quay.

Left A dining area in the San Francisco house of artists Kay Sekimachi and Bob Stocksdale with mid-century vintage pieces.

Below In a 1960s house that has had a contemporary extension, 1950s Harry Betoia chairs sit well with ethnographic artworks.

Opposite In a classically proportioned Copenhagen apartment, the dining room's high ceilings are amplified by the tall double doors and windows. Chairs by Hans Wegner and the plain-form table in light wood have the smooth Scandinavian appeal.

Mid-century design is included in many artful interiors, whether as part of a singular collection or mixed with other periods. The smooth lines and simple forms have proved to have stylish longevity.

Below An Indonesian fan-frame mirror over the French doors emphasizes the height of the room. The gilded fibreglass alligator and Dutch farm table are more favoured objects on display.

Right French furniture designer Jérôme Abel Seguin has spent many years in Indonesia where he is still fascinated by the natural environment and local craft, such as the weaving used to create the cluster chandelier.

Contrasts of rough and smooth, materials that are polished and unworked, and light and dark make for intriguing interiors in minimal contexts.

Right This cool contemporary house keeps to a spare, white theme that is livened up with a collection of large cut vines from Indonesia, an African rug woven of straw and leather, and a chunky wooden table set alongside Magis 'Bombo' chairs.

Left An apartment in a converted warehouse is furnished with an eclectic range of pieces from the antique sideboard to the Verner Panton dining chairs.

Opposite An atmospheric dining room on the ground floor of a German villa where artists Lili Nalovi and Jesko Willert live and work features their own paintings and lampshades.

Right More mixing of styles in a contemporary Oslo apartment in Norway where the traditional antique dresser and dining table are offset by the oversized abstract painting and modernist-style dining chairs. The kitchen is in a niche behind the dresser.

Chandeliers, candlelight and fresh flowers can turn almost any room into an atmospheric dining space.

Above left The top-floor apartment of an antiques collector is a showcase for some of his personal collection, from the carved wooden chair to the Renaissance period turned wood side chairs to the tapestry and the oriental carpet.

Left A renovated farmhouse has been given a more formal dining space which is lined with a collection of antiques belonging to the architect. The antique tapestry sets the background for the space with a glass table and Baroque-style side chairs centred with a large chandelier.

Above Fresh, white table linen, classical-style side chairs and heirloom crystal make a rustic converted barn space into a place for fine dining.

Opposite A curtain from a stage production and a set of busts help to create a theatrical setting for a dinner party. Fresh flowers on the table and strewn through the circular chandelier add to the scene. The curtain also screens a bedroom on the other side.

Above left This summer house situated on the Bosphorus in Istanbul belongs to a very cosmopolitan family and has been a gathering place for generations. The elaborate chandelier is one of many features that have been carefully preserved.

Left A parade of Chippendale chairs and blue-patterned porcelain line the dining room in the home of an architect and antiques collector.

Opposite Built in 1696, this Norwegian farmhouse retains its vivid painted wallcovering from 1760. The chandelier from the famed makers Nøstetangen was specially made for the room at the time.

Large patches of colour on walls, flooring or in paintings add depth and interest to a room, even in an otherwise spare arrangement.

Simple plans and furnishings are sometimes the most welcoming. Deep colours
have greater impact when patterns and ornaments are more restrained.

Opposite In an eighteenth-century Scandinavian coastal retreat the original wall colour has been restored after being found under layers of wallcovering. The white-painted beams and natural plank floor are also in the traditional style.

Above In the Norwegian island home of an artist couple, the simple panelled walls are painted a vivid heritage blue and hung with pictures of sailing ships in reference to the many crafts that can be seen from the windows.

Above right and right More traditional colours and simple furnishings in Scandinavian seaside homes. The lamp by Christine Tønnessen is a gesture to the outdoor inhabitants.

Intimate dining can be in a formal, enclosed space or a corner of an open-plan living area. The recipe calls for soft lighting, warm colours and touches of personal style.

Left The delicate table setting is in keeping with the Gustavian chairs and pendant lamp, panelled woodwork and decorative carpet.

Above The deep-blue stained walls set the intimate mood, along with the darkened still-life. Carved wooden garden benches are used for close seating.

Above Rustic and heritage meet in a modern house with lodge-pole columns, Beidermeier sofa seating and a Native American-inspired painting by Bjørn Ransve.

Right In a minimalist Mallorcan house designed by Claudio Silvestrin, a generous open kitchen area includes a dining table of travertine marble set with Wegner chairs.

Below The home of legendary Finnish designers Vuokko and Antti Nurmesniemi, proponents of the modern movement in the 1960s, was designed by Antti, as were the furnishings.

Opposite Recently renovated, this Estonian apartment building in Tallinn dates from the turn of the nineteenth century. After being empty for several years, the apartment was transformed into an open, loft-style living space. The long dining table borders the kitchen 'cube'. The lamps are from the designers' own 'Shishi' collection.

Left A small, compact kitchen and dining area is made more expansive by a worktop that extends to become a dining table/bar.

Below The zigzag geometry of the glass-framed staircase is a continuous feature in this modern house on three levels. The pendant lamps, table, chairs and cut ferns adhere to a clean minimal approach but with subtle variations in colour and shape which make a more dynamic interior.

Crisp geometry marks a house with modern design. In some rooms all angles are pure, while in others, the lines have softer edges.

Right Architecture firm divA designed this mountain chalet, as well as its custom-made and built-in furnishings. The interior is all wood, while the exterior is predominantly slate.

Below right A tapestry by Jan Groth and chest by Kromata joins an Eero Saarinen Tulip table and Mies van der Rohe side chairs in a classic 1914 Norwegian villa.

A small, functional kitchen space in Provence is brought to life by a pair of Louis XV-style velvet-covered armchairs.

KITCHEN

It is an oft-repeated cliché (is there any other kind?) that the kitchen is the heart of the home. It is the centre, the place where people congregate during odd hours and at family time. Even guests often have to be enticed away by the promise of a cocktail on a sofa, instead of standing at the counter snacking and chatting. The kitchen is also a place for casual and unexpected conversation. After all, it was in a model kitchen that Richard Nixon and Nikita Khrushchev had their famously ill-tempered debate about Communism and fears of Soviet hegemony in 1959.

While it needn't serve as a platform for political strife, one of the most important aspects of a 'real home' must surely be a workable, family-friendly and versatile kitchen space, whether it's a nook set behind the arch of a country house with stone flags and checked curtains, a room framed in old timber with rough plaster walls and kitted out with modern gadgetry or a highly modern design with plenty of signs of use and wear. We have in these pages tiny-sized apartment kitchens and cosy eat-in varieties. There are breakfast nooks, the island, the galley kitchen, the elaborate cook's paradise, but all of the kitchens are real, usable (and well-used) spaces, and their genuine character is easy to perceive.

Of all of the rooms of the house, the evolution of the kitchen is one of the most fascinating developments, along with the bathroom, in terms of the benefits of modernization. Historically, we have gone from cooking, eating and sleeping in the same room to having separate rooms for every function. Some of us have gone back to open-plan spaces where the kitchen is again part of the main living (though not the sleeping) space. When Henry VIII had the kitchens of Hampton Court moved away from the main building because an earlier kitchen fire had scared him, it was awkward for servants who had to cross a courtyard with food they wanted to keep hot. And he wasn't alone in creating work for the staff by locating the kitchen well away from the formal dining spaces.

Today, as most of us do not employ others to cook and serve our food, we look to more practical designs. The well-organized kitchen is like a functioning work of art. And its effect goes far beyond being a place to cook a meal. As a hub of social activity, a kitchen invites interaction. In the

exotic foods and those recipe tomes. This doesn't necessarily call for a high-production space with the most technologically advanced gadgetry, but a place where food can be kept, utensils can be reached, and actually used (and are well organized), where surfaces are not too precious, or overly professional, so they can be worked on, where a cook has the space and the means to create and where people can feel comfortable standing around talking to the chef.

If you're going to spend more time cooking, then other people – your children, your partner, your guests – are going to want to be nearby to keep you company or to ask to sample the dishes. So the hyper-minimal space, without any evidence of food being cooked, a dish being washed or a person being served, is not what we were after here. Neither was it our plan to capture the neo-countrified illusion of a kitchen with stacks of picturesque crockery that never sees a meal or

Antique and modern keep company happily, whether in an old building with pieces of contemporary design or in a new space appointed with a few choice antiques.

UK a genre of fiction, the 'Aga Saga', was named after the large oil-burning stoves. These stories generally follow the domestic anxieties of middle-class families and their local communities. The rubric is telling for the significance of the appliance and the focus on the 'heart' of the home. In real life, as in fiction, the conversation over a cup of tea or a drink at the kitchen table is an intimate one where family and friendships are discussed and brooded over, so the kitchen table is more than just a place to set out food.

In recent years, the popularity of television cooking programmes has made people increasingly aware of healthy eating and of the virtues of eating home-cooked food, as opposed to fast-food or quick, frozen alternatives. They have encouraged people to shop for more fresh produce, to be more creative in their cooking, to try new recipes and foodstuffs, and, of course, to buy more cookery books! But these shows have also made people increasingly conscious and demanding of a well-performing kitchen. They need a place to keep and store all of that produce,

matched swags of calico that come straight from a catalogue. But since more people are coming back into their kitchens, and bringing their family and friends with them, we see more of a personal stamp on the space. It might have a small table and chairs, but they are good modernist design pieces. Or it may have piles of plates and bowls visible, but their colour and pattern will be something worth looking at, and they will look like things that have personal appeal. Our ideal kitchens are those that are practically arranged, using durable materials and yet show a good deal of personal flair.

Achieving this ideal mix can be a challenge, particularly in 'converted' properties. While a lot of us love the idea of preserving the character of an old farmhouse, a historic manor house, a Victorian townhouse or the elements of a light industrial building that has been adapted into fashionable 'lofts', we don't all relish the idea of using the rudimentary kitchen spaces that come with them. There has to be some amount of modern design for a kitchen to be a functional space rather than

a museum piece, and there needs to be some welcoming ambience, good natural light, colour, texture and pleasing details that make the kitchen the rightful heart of the home.

In open-plan spaces, the kitchen can become a conundrum. No one wants to do away with it, but it can dominate a room and become a source of grief if every bit of clutter is always on display. In these pages there are many traditional kitchens but there are also spaces where the kitchen has been cleverly inserted into a larger space. In some cases, the kitchen is arranged along one end of an open space, facing the long wall, for example, so that its impact is minimized. The addition of a multi-functioning partition, such as an open shelf unit, provides a nice line of separation without impeding the flow of light and air. Most open interiors will have some visible structure, such as columns or other supporting elements, and these can be used to mark changes in function. They can also be the point of services, a place to hide water, electrical and ventilation conduits behind some minimal cladding. These are all practical points, but with kitchens it is often the practical that holds back the artful impulses, so it is useful to see how both have been addressed by people who have done so successfully, creating kitchens that we not only admire, but that we can also see ourselves inhabiting.

Even for those who love cooking for themselves, enjoy good design and like to have a kitchen that extends an open invitation to friends and family to participate in the important rituals of cooking and eating together, tastes will vary as to how best to express all of these desires. Luckily, in these pages we have many examples of how to mix modern and historic, minimal and embellished. The numerous creative ways of storing, displaying, illuminating and decorating a kitchen were never so inspiring. Since this isn't a book about pristine worktops and glamorous backdrops for sculptural canapés and equally sculptural people, even the most stylish kitchens here show signs of real life, and the most modest ones display a sense for artful solutions. These are the ways that people have made the warm heart of the kitchen part of the creative heart of the home, where style continues to be important, and colour, art and design are still happily on the menu.

The beauty of small spaces is in light and colour and the few objects that stand out.

Left A modest kitchen in the cabin of an allotment in Oslo contains the basic necessities, as well as a sense of style and tradition.

Above Blue-and-white Portuguese tiles make this kitchen space in the Ile de Ré in France a little moment of beauty.

Right This modest eat-in kitchen shows a wealth of personal touches, from the modern chairs to the worn vintage table and the neatly hung pictures and curios.

Left White walls and flooring and a marble-topped table indicate a place for proper cooking and eating.

Left A French kitchen with a wonderfully tall ceiling and cupboards keeps a familiar country feeling with the chequerboard tiles and open shelves.

Above The wood-panelled cupboards and door suggest a sense of tradition, while the modern furniture and potted herbs show this is a working space.

Opposite A bright London kitchen balances antique furnishings in a pure modern design.

White signals fresh, clean and modern even in older kitchens where occasional antiques and period elements remind us of the past.

Country kitchens extend a warm welcome with sturdy wooden furnishings and an orderly array of small objects and crockery.

The kitchen stove demonstrates its own personality. As more people return to real cooking, their stoves become

symbols of a rediscovered heritage.

The French country kitchen of designer Michel Biehn retains its original terrazzo floor, patterned wall tiles and great chimney piece; the woven chairs are his own design.

A basement kitchen that mixes traditional European elements, such as the tiles, the bread oven, the large hearth and period furniture, with modern and ethnic touches.

Creative re-use is a laudable trend in the modern home. Finding new homes for specialized gear is not only sensible but makes for engaging design.

Opposite The design company Autoban created this fun and functional kitchen area in the corner of a loft space in Istanbul.

Right This wood-lined, cabin-style kitchen contains an antique ice-box, which is still used by the resident.

Above Artist Gerd Verschoor created his own table from a huge slab of hand-cut wood. The bright modern stool chairs and cacophony of cooking utensils suggest a welcoming atmosphere.

Right The kitchen in a converted apartment on the top floor of an old warehouse mixes retro-style pieces with some professional chef's larders for a vintage/industrial look.

Above left A simple small kitchen is a playful space for vintage pieces and pop art.

Left Traditional Dutch tiles.

Above The Provençal country kitchen of an antiques dealer in France has simple tile and stucco walls and cupboards made of painted cast iron. The tiles are eighteenth century.

Above right A new house in South Africa was built to accommodate the large stone boulder, which is a significant presence in the kitchen.

Right From the top-shelf collection of oil lamps to the black-and-white tiles to the cupboard curtain in dyed and printed designs and the geometric floor tiles, this kitchen in an artist's Turkish home is an essay in pattern and colour.

Above left Bright blue paint and white tableware sparkle with the light of the Mediterranean.

Left A kitchen in Provence has been given an original decorative treatment by its artist owner.

Painted walls, cupboards and woodwork liven up the atmosphere of kitchen, storage and eating areas.

Above The kitchen of this Ibiza house is part of a large, open-plan living space on different levels. The storage shelf was made from twigs and its irregular lines complement the rough plaster wall.

Right Vivid colours and a nod to 1950s style give this kitchen a very personal and inviting atmosphere.

Left A series of spice drawers has the charm of a vintage storage cabinet. The metal elements add a slightly industrial edge.

Below and below left A built-in kitchen in formed concrete is made more personal by a collection of ethnic baskets and crockery. The beam across the back wall has been painted with geometric patterns that add some colour in keeping with the neutral background.

Opposite In South Africa this concrete built-in kitchen has been fitted with re-used metal doors. The sharp modern materials contrast nicely with the rough textured walls.

Industrial elements are a popular addition to modern kitchens. Used with other eclectic elements, they add functional integrity and orderly form.

Steel is the ultimate practical surface, bringing a professional, modern quality to a kitchen.

Wood is a material that people love to love. It introduces warmth, texture and beautiful irregularity to a room even alongside more unforgiving surfaces.

Above and opposite This summer house in Estonia is a cornucopia of natural materials, from the woven sapling ceiling work to the tidy logs stored in every compartment to the sturdy log columns and naturally grained carved countertops.

Left A small kitchen area in an arched niche of an open-plan farm building in Normandy. The extra height and large kitchen window are key to making the space feel more expansive.

Right A 'kitchen in a box' created by a designer for his Milan apartment contains everything you need in a tidy and beautifully crafted container made of natural wood. The chevron-patterned floor is a spirited contrast to the plain forms.

Above and right Wood is the perfect modular material and complements even the more industrial-style kitchen elements.

Opposite A kitchen and dining area is tailor made for this large open-plan space in an architect-designed modern penthouse in Oslo. The spiral staircase makes a material intrusion of painted metal.

Shelves display the tools and tableware that symbolize the important ritual of eating together.

Left The elements of storage are made beautiful with painted and glass cabinets, aged wood surfaces and an array of hand-made and vintage bowls, cups, jars and glasses.

Opposite A Danish kitchen combines function with age and everything is tidy in a neat white arrangement.

Displays of collections of crockery, whether they are family heirlooms or flea-market treasures, antique cupboards or distressed cabinetry, imbue a charming country kitchen with real life.

Left A kitchen in an old palace in the centre of Palma, Mallorca, retains its rustic features.

Below White-painted timber cladding signals the breezy atmosphere of this island summer house in Norway.

Left The home of an antiques dealer on Rhode Island, USA, is composed of picturesque vignettes featuring antique and vintage objects.

Opposite In the French countryside near Bordeaux this restored farmhouse belongs to a collector of architectural salvage who prefers objects that have the patina of age.

Rustic utility is a back-to-basics approach that reminds us of simple necessities.

OUTDOOR

One of the greatest legacies of the modernist design tradition is the idea of indoor–outdoor living. This aspect was emphasized by architects such as Mies van der Rohe with his Barcelona Pavilion and by proponents of the International Style, such as Rudolph Schindler and Richard Neutra. Although both Schindler and Neutra came from Austria, a country not known for its warm climate, in the more temperate latitude of southern California they developed an architecture that embraced its setting. They defined not just interior living spaces but also outdoor 'rooms'. Using large sections of glass for entire walls, they allowed the ample vegetation to become part of the atmosphere of the living space of the house. The style often encouraged open-plan arrangements, which meant that the spaces not only flowed into one another but beyond, to the outdoors as well. These houses also included large, overhanging roofs and outdoor paving around the perimeter that created sheltered space just beyond the internal boundary which could be easily integrated into the everyday living area. These ideas have been given new life in the twenty-first century as people are embracing the outdoors as never before in the design and use of their homes. In some cultures this has always been the case, but the most exciting projects here show a renewed appreciation for these outdoor living areas, using comfortable furnishings and a mixture of styles and approaches to create outdoor spaces that are as full of personal style and taste as their indoor counterparts.

Most people, no matter where they live, want to have some kind of outdoor living space. This can be a small apartment balcony or patio or a rambling terrace with various seating arrangements, lounges and a grand swimming pool. It can be a long loggia with built-in benches covered in ethnic fabrics or an enclosed porch, as is often seen in Nordic homes, a space to admire the landscape and surroundings no matter what the weather is like. One way of making a small house feel more expansive is by opening it up to the outdoors, incorporating the surrounding landscaping into livable area. For example, a house might have an extended terrace, something that has been done in Mediterranean countries for centuries. This effect can also be achieved with a large pergola providing shade and shelter in a patio area, covered in vines and aromatic plants. Or a house might have a paved terrace set in a more formal garden with topiary, ornamental stonework and ponds. In these places the judicious planting of fragrant varieties of trees and shrubs will provide shade from intense sun and will also bathe the space in natural perfume.

In addition to European examples, Islamic architecture gives us wonderful ideas for outdoor spaces. One only needs to conjure the Alhambra in Granada, Spain, with its enchanting patios and richly tiled open rooms, or the Alcázar in Seville, with its extended gardens, reflecting pools and fountains. The delicate splash of water or the sound of small inlets of running water add an audible pleasure to the senses. The best modern architecture draws on all of these traditions to construct indoor spaces that engage with the natural setting, offer the most pleasing views available and provide the best balance of shade and solar gain, while also allowing for an easy transition from indoor to outdoor living.

Many European countries have strong traditions of formal garden landscaping, incorporating sculpted hedges, parterres, statuary, fountains and other ornaments. These need not be the model for every outdoor space, but they certainly bring us back to the idea that orchestrating the natural setting has been on our domestic agenda for a long time. Nowadays, just because someone is living in a cottage instead of a castle or a streamlined

Opposite above Old vines frame
a seating and bar area of a
traditional pale blue house in Ibiza.

Opposite below In Provence,
a stone-paved courtyard patio
is set with a quintessentially
French garden style, white-painted
wrought-iron chairs set beneath
a white umbrella. The thick mass
of the house promises cooler
temperatures inside.

Right A Scandinavian outdoor
scene with a sheltered entrance to
the enclosed courtyard. The neatly
stacked wood means that when
the mercury drops, a warm fire is
never far away.

minimal house instead of a traditional villa, it does not mean that the outdoor space cannot be an attractive and well-integrated part of a scheme that includes both house and garden.

When we speak of 'outdoor rooms' we are talking about spaces that are organized, furnished, shaded and otherwise made hospitable for sitting with friends, lounging, relaxing with a book, sun-bathing or dining al fresco. There are lots of different ways to articulate these kinds of rooms, using furniture and sometimes larger elements such as garden walls, pergolas, canopies and screens. It always seems very civilized to find an outdoor area set out and furnished almost as comfortably as a well-appointed sitting room. This has been

A comfortable seat in the sun or in the cool shade, these are the few instances we allow ourselves just to sit and gaze outwardly and enjoy the view.

the model in some countries for centuries, but it can still be updated and adapted in many new ways. Covered cushions instead of hard seating, table cloths and other textiles, some candles, a lantern or some fanciful garden lights, even a woven mat underfoot: these are the things that make an outdoor space really livable and most are simple and inexpensive. The only luxury we can't all depend on is the weather.

However, even in colder climates some people just seem to know how to live outdoors with little effort. In Scandinavian countries, outdoor rooms are used even in winter, with some heating and blankets provided. The tradition of the outdoor sauna and hot tub comes from places where colder weather is the norm. And where the heat is so intense as to drive people indoors, houses have long been adapted with large, shaded patios. Here we have examples of the Moorish style or the *riad*, with their enclosed courtyards, beautiful ornamental tiles and flowing water. We show shaded terraces set out with built-in benches covered in traditional textiles or a wide bed draped in mosquito netting for a refreshing afternoon rest. The desert cultures use the courtyard model as well, while in milder climates a combination of sun and shade, wind-

breaks, enclosures and open vistas are used to make the most of the possibilities for outdoor living in conjunction with the orientation and daily movement of the sun. Some houses might have a terrace on either side, to take the sun at morning in one spot and in the afternoon in another, or to retreat away from it in opposing directions. The point is that the outdoor space has been planned to take best advantage of the position and views and as a result more time can be spent comfortably outside, enjoying the warmth, the breeze, the garden or forest and a sense of the natural environment.

Although some of us view gardens or terraces as places purely for lounging or relaxation, more of the daily rituals of cooking and eating can be enjoyed in the open air as well. In these pages are Mediterranean houses with fully functioning outdoor cooking facilities, a Norwegian cabin with an outdoor kitchen and another in Turkey. There are proper dining tables and chairs in painted wrought iron; there are rough-hewn picnic tables and ornamental tea tables. There are enclosed courtyards, sheltered verandahs, stone-paved garden terraces and tiled corner patios. Not all of the inhabitants shown here are keen gardeners but for those who are, the arrangements outside are as carefully managed as they are inside. Even those in harsher climates find ways to indulge their passions for gardening by making the best use of enclosed garden rooms for planting and growing.

In all of these a discernible sense of style is combined with objects of personal value to achieve a relaxed, comfortable and captivating effect. These are not the most elite or exclusive residences of the rich and famous, but some of the best planned and most inviting, whether because of the arrangements of furnishings, ethnic and modern, traditional and contemporary, high style or handmade. Some outdoor spaces are incredibly well-manicured, tidy presentations, others have a more natural, overgrown abundance. But the universal appeal is a certain combination of beautiful surroundings, with a well-directed view, and furnishing, lighting and decoration that give the idea that here is a place for living and relaxing, for dining and entertaining, for indulging in the everyday pleasures that make the life of a house extend beyond solid walls.

Left The old stone walls contrast with the sharp lines of the modern pergola. The canvas curtains make a clever and easy enclosure from wind or low sun.

Above An old cistern has been preserved at this Ibiza house. A simple lounger and a pot of bright flowers turn an antique view into an inviting spot.

Right Adirondack chairs on the wood-planked verandah face towards the view. A fabric curtain offers protection from the wind and the sun.

Below left Simple canvas covers turn an impromptu patio set-up into a proper dining space.

Below right An Adirondack-inspired chair set beneath the shade of a wide palm offers a moment of relaxation.

Al fresco dining shouldn't be a rarified pleasure. Food and drink always taste better outdoors, in the shade of lush leafy trees, touched by the breeze and with a view through the natural landscape.

Left A Norwegian cottage built with local stones from a nearby beach uses minimal resources, but provides generous comforts, including an outdoor kitchen.

Above and opposite Setting a table in the pocket of greenery. Trees and hedges provide natural shade, while the table linen offers a bit of sophistication.

Right The ingredients for the perfect outdoor dining experience, a commodious table beneath a lush pergola, a chilled bottle of wine and a lovely view.

Below right Scandinavian summers offer plenty of opportunity for eating and relaxing outdoors.

Left Making the most of natural vegetation and traditional white-washed walls, this Ibiza terrace has a very rustic minimal appeal.

Below left The coastal experience of this house was enhanced by adding a deck overlooking a rocky promontory and the wider Mediterranean.

Below A built-in outdoor dining table ensures that the party can always be taken outside.

Above A summer house in Turkey with a complete outdoor kitchen beneath the shelter of the extended roof.

Right Vivid painted colours and bright vegetation in a well-shaded outdoor dining space for a house in the Balearic Islands.

Shade and a cool corner under a canopy, umbrella or a vine-covered pergola are essential to a relaxing outdoor space.

Above Architect Antonia Obrador added this large pavilion to an old stone house in Mallorca. Antique Mallorcan lemonwood sofas and chairs are arranged around the terrace and a wood-burning stove is positioned at the edge.

Left The broken paving of this Provençal terrace makes an enclosed garden 'room' beneath the shade of mature trees and a dining umbrella.

Opposite left Shaded spots for outdoor eating are created using a combination of umbrellas and existing natural covering. White-painted furniture makes a classic garden picture, and weathered wood has the patina of many summers.

Right Tall plane trees and a white canvas canopy wrapped around massive old vines create a protective corner for drinks or dining on this terrace in southern France.

Classical garden scenes from France, Spain and Norway show a modern taste for weathered stonework, antique fountains and ornamental balustrades all draped in swags of natural greenery.

Above left A cloistered room shows its Moorish heritage in the pointed arches and patterned window screens.

Left Nineteenth-century scrolled wrought-iron furniture offers diners a view through courtyard arches to the sea beyond.

Above Untreated sandstone blocks were used to create a more modernist form in an area of traditionally Moorish architecture. The terrace cloister is retained in this more rectilinear building.

Opposite Beautiful etched plasterwork and fretted screens in a *riad* atrium in Morocco. Traditional jars, a square seat and an inlaid table ornament the perfect spot for a glass of mint tea.

Islamic Spain offers some of the most enchanting examples of well-designed outdoor spaces that are integral to the buildings, landscape and lifestyle.

Modern indoor–outdoor design features oversized windows and door openings that allow for easy movement between spaces. A view through the living space will naturally draw visitors outwards.

Opposite Sharp minimalism as designed by Claudio Silvestrin in Mallorca extends sharp planes into the verdant surroundings.

Left An elegant terrace designed by the legendary architect/builder Sverre Fehn overlooks a forested valley in Norway.

Below In Portugal the garden of a small farmhouse is set for hot weather with cushions on an old wooden lounger and a stone trough formerly used for animals re-purposed as a plunge pool.

Contemporary hard-scaping renders an outdoor space into a sophisticated sculptural form in the landscape. The sharp edges are softened by abundant greenery.

Left Colonial-inspired wooden and woven seating, Moorish-style wall lamps, classical clay jars and potted plants create a comfortable seating area on a covered brick terrace in Ibiza.

Below left In Scandinavia outdoor living isn't just for warm weather. Here kilim-covered cushions and sheepskin throws offer a bit of a place to warm up outside.

Below In South Africa, a covered porch has been made into a welcoming outdoor space with a natural-woven mat, a barrel table, Craftsman-style chairs and sofa and plenty of cushions covered in local woven fabrics.

Opposite above A well-furnished loggia features Mallorcan antiques and brightly coloured fabrics and objects.

Opposite below Here the brightness comes from the painted exterior wall, which contrasts with the neutral furnishings and proliferating vegetation.

Lounging is one of the most pleasurable activities in a well-appointed outdoor space. Furnishings can be soft and comfortable and placed in a space with warming sun or refreshing shade.

The siesta is a southern European and Latin American tradition, but the benefits of an afternoon rest are pretty universal. In the hot afternoons, a place for peaceful repose need only be quiet and calming.

Above left The irregular stonework of this rustic mountain home has been made more hospitable with specially designed cushions, a simple kilim rug and minimal decoration.

Left A built-in day-bed is tucked away out of the sun on a small terrace that also contains a table and chair for more upright pursuits.

Above A rustic hideaway from the midday sun was built into the hillside. The stone platforms used as a bed and banquette are covered in traditional Mallorcan fabric.

Opposite There is plenty of room to stretch out comfortably on this low bed in a corner of a patio in Spain. The tile floor and seating are covered in traditional textiles.

Huts and garden rooms make the 'outdoor room' a physical construction in which the aim is to be as open as possible to the elements, but sheltered from the extremes.

Above A classic Norwegian enclosed verandah can be opened up on warmer days or closed against inclement weather, while still allowing sun into the space.

Far left A diminutive but important space for the owners to indulge their 'green fingers'.

Left An old-fashioned glass-enclosed space can be either a 'winter garden' or a 'sun porch'.

Opposite Sheltered from the sun and wind but open to outdoor pleasures, this little poolside house in Provence offers the perfect midday refuge.

Left The northern Europeans love to be out in nature, but they have also learned to be practical. This boathouse in Norway offers seaside dining with large timber doors that can be opened for a wide view of water and sky.

Right The snug painted timber alcove is one of many sheltered outdoor spaces surrounding a wind-swept island location in Finland.

Below In New England, the architect Ross Anderson has built a small country house inspired by vernacular barn buildings. Sliding doors on both sides of the house open the interior to the views and fresh air of the outdoors.

In this work space created in the open-plan living area of a converted church in the Hudson Valley, New York, the desk, shelves and chair were made by the owner, craftsman Chris Lehrecke. The pure wood forms and pale background retain some of the spare quality of the old church.

WORK

Those of us with contemporary 'live-work' spaces may think of ourselves as very modern with our fast Wi-Fi connections and our wafer-thin laptops ready for action anywhere around the house. But the house as a place of work is nothing new. In the Middle Ages, houses were usually also places of work, as well as places for communal gathering and shelter for employees, servants, apprentices, extended family, anyone attached to the house/workplace who needed somewhere to eat and sleep. And this use carried on in some places through the nineteenth century. Madame Bovary, the nineteenth-century anti-heroine of Flaubert's most famous novel, lives in the same house where her doctor husband practises medicine. 'What makes it especially convenient for a doctor', the pharmacist explains, 'is a door onto the Lane, which makes it possible to come and go without being seen.' Charles Dickens' novels are full of quirky shopkeepers and rough-and-ready publicans who live above or behind their places of work. Dickens also gave us poor old Bob Cratchit, who sits uncomfortably on his clerk's stool in the unheated office of Scrooge and Marley, a bleak image of desk work indeed.

Later in the nineteenth century, people began to separate their home and work place and even the location from where they worked. Those who could afford to moved happily to houses out of the city, where their jobs or businesses were based, into new,

quiet residential suburbs. Many people still speak of the importance of keeping a clean separation between home and work.

In some ways we seem to have come full circle, with internet and computer services making possible new, more flexible working *from home*. Nowadays, what we mean by our 'home office' areas are much more sophisticated, of course, than in previous centuries. They are also more private, combining the technology of the high-spec office and the personal trappings of home. And as working from home becomes increasingly commonplace, people are becoming more deliberate about how they arrange their home work space.

In these pages we look at different interpretations of work spaces at home. Some are just a little desk in a corner of a room, for sorting through post or having a quick look on the laptop. Others are more elaborate office set-ups, with proper desk space and shelves. Still other people have created 'studio' spaces, with larger tables for laying out fabrics, drawings or other materials or for having creative meetings. And then there are the home libraries, whether traditional rooms lined with shelves full of books or spaces where books stand on floors and other surfaces.

It seems that people are no longer ashamed of having a work space at home or they don't see it as a space that is just left as a second thought. Nowadays, though some still want to hide the clutter of office equipment, many people want a work space that is less transient and more comfortable, even part of the living space. Of course, the more serious home-worker might require a designated room, as opposed to a little table space, something that can't be contained easily in an open-plan environment but is better accommodated away from public areas, somewhere with a door that can be shut. However, many home work spaces can be, and are, much more flexible.

Flexible too are the furnishings used to create the functional work place at home. Some who work from home are not satisfied simply to add a desk and a filing cabinet to a spare corner, they are looking for more salubrious fixtures and fittings. In doing so, they are finding they need not adhere to any formula for what a work space should look and feel like. Unlike a public office space with uniform chairs, partitions and uniformly lacklustre inspiration, a place for working at home can be enriched with personal taste and character. All the things that might make the task of working at home more pleasurable are to be encouraged, whether it's beautifully patterned draperies in your 'office' window, an ornamental mirror over your desk or an array of wonderful prints or sketches to draw your eye to a spot of beauty. While the typical commercial office space might allow a few family photos and a single-stem vase, at home you can indulge in a wall of images and a great spray of flowers to awaken your senses and your mind.

A personal office space at home has no restrictions on what can be used, so it need not be so banal as the cubicle nor as torturous as Cratchit's stool. Banished are metal-and-wood-veneer desks and plastic chairs, although some of the modernist masterpieces have pride of place in the new 'home' offices and studios. In some of the most inspired (and inspiring) work spaces, people have taken old furnishings and adapted them to new uses. Instead of a drab office chair, why not, as some people have done here, use a comfortable upholstered side chair, a simple plank wood chair from Indonesia, a classic modernist Danish armchair or an eighteenth-century French *fauteuil*? In the twenty-first century, as we rethink previous demands for disposable furniture, many people are considering old pieces of furniture with a creative eye and wondering what new use they could be adapted to, and the work space is the perfect place to be creative with utility.

Of course, there is the abiding question of storage. If you want to have a work space that doesn't become a corner full of clutter, there will need to be filing cabinets, or perhaps not. Maybe an antique dresser will suffice, an apothecary's cabinet or a vintage chest originally meant for storing and displaying jewelry. Bookshelves might be in a tidy row over your desk or they might cover entire walls. Some rooms here feature books stacked in artful piles along the wall. Some bookshelves not only span the walls, but also continue over doors and up the stairs. Then there are the 'book' shelves in name only, used by makers in creative fields for holding an assortment of fabrics or art supplies or

Seemingly awkward spaces can offer great opportunities for creating compact and distinctive work areas. Rethinking understairs cupboards, unlikely corners and architectural elements can solve spatial problems and present new ideas for storage and access.

Materials matter as they add to the atmosphere of a space. The white-painted brick of a loft space, the corrugated metal of an agricultural shed, the refined wood of an ornamental chair help to create a distinctive and inspiring environment.

Opposite A loft space in South Africa with plank wood floors and painted brick walls features a desk area overlooked by a collection of odd-shaped mirrors.

Above This renovated stable has become an office, but the metal siding is a reminder of its farming heritage.

Right The work-table in a designer's Parisian apartment holds a book of sketches. The rush-seated chair has an intricate, Chinoiserie-style frame.

for displaying crockery that might have just come from the kiln.

Deciding where to put a work space usually depends on how much 'work' needs to be done. In the following pages, some houses feature proper office spaces that can be kitted out with all of the necessary trappings and closed off for privacy. Others have designated an area of the open-plan living area – as in a converted church in New England or in a South African loft – for desk work. Some people have managed to convert seemingly unusable spaces under the stairs or roof gable into a stylish hive of productivity. In some of the most striking vignettes, a single piece of furniture, the poetic little writing desk, sits waiting to inspire a letter (possibly even handwritten) or a few thoughtful verses. Some workers at home need proper pedestal desks with drawers on either side, while others prefer a pretty little escritoire with its irresistibly charming array of compartments. Still others have adapted tables – some antique and decorative, others modern and functional – to office purposes. Jane Austen wrote most of her novels sitting at a tiny circular side table in the window of the parlour, so creativity and efficiency are certainly not dependent on the size of the work space.

As in most areas of the house, natural light is also essential to a work area. Perhaps it is more essential, as our brains respond specifically to the stimulus of natural light. A work space, for example, that receives a healthy dose of morning sunlight is sure to provide more motivation than a darkened room. And good circulation of air is also crucial to keeping the mind sharp.

One of the most fascinating aspects of the work spaces photographed here is the sense of intimacy they portray, especially those that feature little curios, collections or quirky containers for a desk or artistic accessories. Most are mixes of styles and periods, and most include some sort of curious object or piece of furniture that tells you this actually belongs to someone. Nothing is perfectly matched or uniformly arranged but every example has some element that catches the eye and makes us want to linger a moment longer in that space and perhaps be inspired to create.

Right A recycled industrial unit works as an organizing tool.

Left In the little mezzanine office in artist Kay Sekimachi's studio an old Japanese chest provides storage and another surface to display her small, delicate pieces.

Opposite In the Indonesian home office of designer Jérôme Abel Seguin, papers are kept in a tidy display, rather than being filed, for quick reference. The rough-hewn bench offers more space for laying out work.

Studio space differs somewhat from regular office or work space, implying a more creative component and the need for space for laying out fabrics, paintings or works of art, as well as storing a range of supplies.

Opposite Pastels and pretty patterns fill the home studio of Tone Finnanger, the young Norwegian creator of popular Tilda hobby books.

This page Kay Sekimachi needs lots of open vertical space to work on her intricate weavings in her top-floor studio near San Francisco.

Opposite A former outbuilding on a French farm has been converted into a spacious studio for creating the artist's distinctive textiles and wallcoverings.

Right Featuring a classic Arne Jacobsen 'Ant' chair, this is a cool, modern work space.

Below left An old Spanish *finca* demonstrates a rich array of inspiration.

Below right This clean, light-filled studio space belies its situation in Paris.

Integrated work spaces that sit in full view make this area part of the atmosphere of the house, a signal that the creative mind is at work.

Desks can inspire almost lyrical praise from the people who choose, own and work from them. They are not just furnishings but hubs of inspiration.

Opposite above left An attic space with lots of natural light is used as both a sitting area and small work space. An absence of clutter makes the lower ceiling height less oppressive.

Opposite above right In an old Nordic home, Danish modernist furniture and an antique iron stove create a warm welcome.

Opposite below left The desk in this Californian house can be closed up and baskets used for storage, so a work space blends with the living area.

Opposite below right In a home office overlooking dramatic cliffs down to the sea, a desk made of travertine and granite connects with the rocky scenery.

Right This small tidy desk area is functional and unobtrusive in a house where transparency is key.

Left In a French townhouse that has been restored to preserve its original features, an antique, painted secretaire is used in the corner of the master bedroom.

Opposite above left A secretaire of Scandinavian provenance makes a small office in the corner of an enclosed verandah.

Opposite above right In a New England farmhouse, a tall, painted American heritage-style bookshelf-desk creates a writing corner.

Opposite below left A sunny alcove off the kitchen has been made into a simple office area with a vintage knee-hole desk and a rush-seated side chair.

Opposite below right In a well-preserved Georgian townhouse in London the office space has a very modern appeal.

Above left An Empire burlwood secretaire is paired with a Philippe Starck chair.

Above right The home office area of a converted barn is dominated by a giant floral spray.

Left In the tiled entrance of a restored Ibiza house an antique Spanish stretcher-legged table becomes an elegant desk.

Opposite An eighteenth-century Norwegian house is filled with original decorative paintwork which is also displayed on the enchanting secretaire-cabinet.

Right A little slant-top desk sits below some antique paintings for inspiration.

Below The ornate table and chair contrast with the rustic dining table beyond in a Scandinavian manor house.

Left This restored townhouse in Provence has been kept spare so the textured walls and terracotta floor have a greater impact. The desk is in a shaded corner of the living space.

Right A collector of eighteenth-century French textiles has created a period vignette with an old portrait, a dainty escritoire and ribbon-tied piles of fabric.

Below The slant-top desk is the perfect display space for this vintage telephone.

Opposite A writing desk positioned in a corner of a kitchen in Provence is perfectly sited to receive natural light from the window and warmth from the old stone fireplace.

Right This simply furnished office corner in an Ibiza house focuses on the modern desk and chair and the traditional tile floor.

Below The blue-painted window frames correspond to the tones of the kilim rug. An antique pine pedestal desk reflects the somewhat rustic flavour of the interior.

Above In a Mexican house, large timber doors open from a courtyard to a spacious work area.

'A room without books is like a body without a soul', as Cicero once said. Whether set out in neat, logical arrangements, displayed across entire walls or stacked in artful piles on the floor, books enrich the life of a room.

Left A tiny, book-lined chamber off the bedroom of a preserved French townhouse is a magical little retreat.

Above The layers of wood in the sculpture, right, are echoed in the array of spines along the shelves.

Right Here the antique trestle-table, painted armchair and march of books along the walls create a haven for quiet thought.

Right The stacks of books in this art-filled Parisian apartment are like an installation.

Below right A secretaire has been built into a wall of books in a home library warmed by natural light.

A local Mallorcan craftsman
was called in to create this
unique staircase and alcove.
The curvaceous design is
reminiscent of the organic forms
of Art Nouveau and the elaborate
turn-of-the-century designs by
Antoni Gaudí in Barcelona.

STAIRS

It is still considered to be possible that Leonardo da Vinci had a hand in designing the French Renaissance château of Chambord. If so, then it was he who came up with the magnificent double-helical staircase that forms the spectacular centre of the hall. Rising up three storeys, the twisting pair of stairs mirror one another but never meet. Openings in each side allow guests on opposite flights of stairs to glimpse each other at points along the journey, but enter and exit the stairs completely on their own. An opening in the roof topped with a sort of lighthouse structure lets natural light down through the white stone core.

Even without such complex architectural feats, many a dramatic entrance has been contrived with the sweep of a grand stair, or two. Film directors love a good staircase for setting scenes of high drama, glamour and romance. We all like to see a well-staged chase scene on stairs. We think of Scarlett O'Hara swanning down that plush red staircase in *Gone with the Wind*, also being carried up it, and then finally, sinking down onto a lower step and becoming philosophical about her future without Rhett. In *Vertigo* the staircase produces a paralysing sense of disorientation and fear. And then there is the grand staircase of the Spanish Colonial Revival mansion in *Sunset Boulevard*. Norma Desmond, the iconic washed-up and deluded film star, imagines that she is acting an iconic scene as she descends the tall, curving stairs to be engulfed

Functional is a term that we associate with stairs, both as a means of helping us move between floors and as the landings, levels and hollows become spaces for storage, display and organization.

in a sea of camera lights and eager reporters. In fiction, and later in film, J. K. Rowling took the bewildering nightmare (and art) of a moving staircase and made it part of everyday life at Hogwarts.

Stairs also inspire a sense of mystery – where do they lead? In contrast to the grand staircase, a small or hidden staircase makes a more secretive passage, a place for intrigue and assignations. Ghosts are reported to spend a lot of time wafting up or down stairs, or brooding at the top or bottom. Countless mystery novels, fashion shoots, scenes of grand balls and musical dance routines couldn't exist without good stairs.

Our day-to-day relationship with stairs may not be so dramatic, but we use them for many things other than getting from one floor to the next. They are there for sitting on, for setting things down, from a cup of coffee on the way out the door to piles of the morning post. Who among us has not had the childhood pleasure of sliding down banisters and peeking through railings when one is meant to be in bed? On outdoor stairs we set out potted plants or garden statuary. And in considering the look and feel of a home interior we often see stairs not just as functional elements but as contributions to the interior design scheme.

Here we look at stairs that could easily be part of a creative film or stage set, and others that look and feel utterly utilitarian, though still in some way pleasant and interesting in their own context. The style of a staircase usually reflects the age and architectural style of the house, though it is not unheard of to make a modern insertion into an older building, especially where a conversion to new use has taken place.

In the following interiors the stairs show an array of styles, designs and approaches which will quickly dispel any notion that stairs are simple utilitarian gestures. From old farmhouses to modern apartments to architect-designed villas, the size, material and position of this basic functional element shows impressive and inspiring variations. There are enclosed stairs that lead from the public living space to the private upper floors, and open stairs that display themselves as works of geometric elegance. There are traditional timber

stairs with painted steps, risers and rails and natural wooden stairs that appear as sculptural paeans to that material.

There are stairs that become storage and those that seem meant to stand completely alone and untouched by everyday life. There are highly decorative stairs that make an undeniable design statement, adorned with decorative tiles, swirling balustrades and scrolled railings, and there are others that are designed to have little impact except to make as light an intrusion as possible.

While some staircases are kept away from the main areas of circulation, others are a celebration of design skill set beneath a central corridor of natural light. Some make clever twists and turns, while

bringing light down through the intervening floors. Treads made of glass are also possible, though not very common, creating stairs that are a towering prism of light. In an open-plan arrangement a glazed partition can allow light to pass through the stair column rather than being blocked by a solid wall. A stairway that is lit from above helps to maintain that pleasant atmosphere of uninterrupted natural light throughout the space. If it has open treads then it becomes even less substantial.

Stairs are sometimes described as being sculptural and there are several examples here that meet that criteria, whether it is a uniform set of gently curved railings in polished metal, a slim zigzag of steel ascending in an open space or stepped

Timber stairs have a particular appeal both for the material and for a kind of nostalgia. There is something comforting about the occasional creak, the feel of worn planks on bare feet. Painted wooden stairs with the reassuring patina of age recall the comforts of a simpler life.

others have been carefully designed with treads that, rather than resting on a framework of risers, are made to cantilever from an anchor in the wall so that they appear to float in space.

Heavier stairs of stone and tile are sometimes offset with finer iron railings that also allow the shape and design of the stairs to be visible in a single beguiling swirl. Here also are some rooms accessed by only the simplest of devices, a wooden box stair or even just a timber ladder, which has a very different but still significant impact on a room.

While timber is a favourite material for staircases, and stone is frequently found in the stairs of historic properties, especially in the warmer climates of the Mediterranean, it is glass and steel that have freed stairs from encumbrance. Cantilevered treads are often in steel, which can be manufactured in thin plates that offer a slender profile, while still able to guarantee strength and durability. Glass used either as a balustrade or to provide a transparent enclosure allows natural light to penetrate the stairwell. This is particularly effective when a skylight is in place at the top level,

low concrete partition that ascends alongside the treads, making a pure pattern of geometry. A staircase in a Mallorcan house designed by a local craftsman is sculpture in stone, its curves echoing the organic forms of Art Nouveau.

The spiral staircase is still a popular bit of functionalism, taking up much less floor space than a straight staircase or a wider revolving staircase, and certainly less intrusive than an open sweep of stairs. However, looking here, we can see that the circular staircase has also been reworked in dynamic modern forms that are much more than pieces of utilitarian architecture.

And still there are the grand hall stairs, those sweeping gestures of elegance, glamour and romance that we all respond to and which film-makers have indulged us with on so many occasions. We mostly associate them with old houses that were more concerned with aesthetics than with efficiency. In a real home they are both beautiful and fit for use, the way anything in an ideal arrangement should be.

Bespoke stairs are intriguing for their unusual shapes, context and materials. They remind us that stairs are a utilitarian element in a house, but also a creative one.

Rustic is a word that implies rough-hewn but also 'honesty' and 'integrity'.

Opposite A stone cottage in Estonia has been preserved with all of its rustic charm. The loft is accessed from the spare dining room by a simple timber ladder.

Above In a former mill building, dating from the nineteenth century, the original wooden stairs still function beautifully.

Right The stripped timber floors and timber features of this restored farmhouse complement a collection of found objects and furnishings.

Below Pattern is the abiding principle in this South African home where floors, stairs and furnishings reflect the resident's eye for design.

Above The curved stone stairs of an old French townhouse proudly wear their age.

Left An artist's Provençal retreat reflects his passion for pattern and colour.

Opposite The beautiful simplicity of these stone stairs in a house in Palma on Mallorca are highlighted by the delicate iron balustrade.

Grand entrances hardly come any grander than those with a tall, sweeping staircase to draw attention upwards and emphasize the volume of a large hall.

Decorative stairways are like evolving masterpieces in the heart of a living space. Every journey reveals another detail to be admired and a procession of vantage points.

Opposite above The brass finial of a scrolled banister stands out against the patterned marble floor.

Opposite below The double staircase in this entrance hall in Turkey beckons exploration.

Above An elegant polished wooden staircase curls between the floors of a French manor house on the west coast.

Above right Simple ironwork railings follow the preserved stone stairway, which rises steeply through a Parisian townhouse.

Right This grand stone staircase in Turkey, with a carved balustrade in an interlocking loop pattern, is covered with a long boldly patterned floor runner.

As architectural elements, stairs can become a way of carrying through a larger design aesthetic, whether it is something modern, high-tech, historic or an expression of craft.

Opposite above left In a top-floor, open-plan space a staircase made of a single sheet of metal makes a minor intrusion.

Opposite above right Open-tread metal stairs with a glass partition allow light to travel through this open-plan space.

Opposite below left This staircase made of metal grating and wood in a basement apartment has a modern industrial quality.

Opposite below right A Parisian loft designed by architect Pascal Cheikh Djavadi has been made more dynamic with skewed geometric elements and a 'floating' staircase.

Right An open-plan interior in Ibiza features a polished concrete floor and a cast-concrete staircase. The timber screen hides a sound system.

This page Thin metal rails and open treads allow the free flow of views and natural light.

Opposite Stair treads in blue glass reflect on the polished concrete floor and echo the hues of the sea which is visible through floor-to-ceiling windows.

The spiral staircase has come in and out of fashion. But there is something about the fine, sinuous twist of metal that speaks of glamour and modernity.

The bedroom of a restored palace in Mallorca features a Mallorcan-designed bed with scrolled decoration. Muted sunlight washes over the floor laid in traditionally patterned tiles.

BEDROOM

The most private room in the house shouldn't be about decorating trends, but about comfort and sanctuary. Yet most people who have a sense of style will feel happier in a room that reflects their awareness of design, whether it is the sitting room, the kitchen or the place where they go to bed at night. Of course, some see a bedroom not only as a room for sleep, but also one for relaxing, reading, lounging, or even enjoying breakfast and the newspaper on a Sunday, especially if the room extends to a terrace or balcony. The master suite will include a private bathing area, which in some more modern arrangements might consist of a freestanding bath next to the fireplace or a bathroom that is only separated by a partition. There might also be a dressing area, a comfortable chair or an upholstered chaise longue, or even a writing desk tucked into a corner.

In the days when the elite kept their own private apartments within the larger palace or royal residence, the bedroom had many functions and could even be available for intimate meetings and conversation. Nowadays we tend to keep our bedrooms more to ourselves, but there are some bedrooms – guest bedrooms and children's rooms – which will be seen by visitors. Each has a distinct purpose and decorative sensibility, but in all cases in the house that is both stylish and organized for real living the bedrooms will reflect the same creative mix of elements as the other

Sanctuary is something we love to find in our own bedroom, the low light, the calm atmosphere, the soft fabrics to aid peaceful relaxation.

living spaces. However, in the master suite, personal tastes are usually indulged a little more than in the public rooms.

At Monticello, the house Thomas Jefferson designed for himself, his bed was in an alcove between two rooms. The alcove was open at both sides, so that he could step directly from his bed into either his dressing area or, if struck by sudden inspiration, his office, where he kept such innovations as a copying instrument with two pens, one to write with and one to copy as he wrote. Both rooms are lit by large skylights and are less intimate and more open than many people would now prefer. But the bedroom, like the rest of the house, reflects Jefferson's love of classical architecture, with its minimal ornament and generous proportions.

At the sixteenth-century château de Chenonçeau in the Loire there are several elaborately decorated bedrooms. Among them is one lined in dark, carved panelling and huge Flemish tapestries with a lavish four-poster bed that belonged to the formidable Catherine de Medici, wife of Henry II of France. Another is swathed in pale blue velvet and belonged to Diane de Poitiers, the king's mistress, to whom Henry presented the château as a gift. There is also a 'Bedroom of the Five Queens' meant to welcome the royal daughters and daughters-in-law.

These examples are given not to suggest that the modern bedroom should strive to emulate the spectacular palaces of old, but to demonstrate how very different ideas are brought to bear even in a room dedicated mainly for prolonged periods of sleeping. Although our bedrooms are less about demonstrations of status than those examples, even today there are all kinds of rituals associated with going to sleep, such as reading or writing in bed, dressing, bathing and perhaps some form of meditation or relaxation. And there are those rituals we perform when we wake, such as trying to open the room to as much natural light as possible to help us switch on our minds for the day ahead. Having a sleeping environment that is pleasant, calming, comfortable and a pleasure to wake in is one of the most essential elements of a home interior.

It goes without saying that the bed itself is the primary focus of the room. In this chapter we

a long love, deepens with time
May Sarton 1976

Above left A room in a converted monastery retains its pure atmosphere, though the carved bed and trinkets create a livelier mood.

Left An Umbrian house with fresco-painted walls has the look and feel of an old Italian palazzo.

Above This old stone house in Provence has been restored but the ceiling beams and arched window openings have been preserved.

have beds that are grand affairs, swathed in draped canopies and covered in rich fabrics. Some have intricately carved wooden bedsteads and others are antiques with wood canopies and hangings like those used in past centuries. Some are large, 'fit for a king', others are modestly cosy. Some people even prefer monastic simplicity. One of the most famous beds in history, the Great Bed of Ware, was made in around 1690, and is over three metres (11 ft) wide and two metres (7½ ft) long. It was built not for a royal palace, but for an English inn. It is a full four-poster bed of carved oak, topped with a wooden canopy featuring an elaborate decorative frieze, and is now owned by the Victoria and Albert Museum in London. None of the beds shown here approach such extravagance, but the idea of a bed that is a singular indulgence is still some people's idea of paradise.

In addition to being a place for rest, the bedroom has a special identity as a very private retreat. Some examples here present a sophisticated arrangement of modern furnishings, while others have been created by people who want to be surrounded by favourite works of art. Some people embrace the romantic sensibility in designing their sleeping quarters. Soft lighting and silky fabrics, a chandelier perhaps and that ultimate accessory, a wood-burning fire, all add to the feeling of romance. Of course, bedrooms aren't only used at night and the effect of natural light changes the character and mood of a room immediately. A skylight or French doors bring in morning sun and open a room to daytime use. There is something about being able to walk directly from the bedroom to a balcony or terrace that speaks of luxury even if it is only a small space. Nowadays, many people who travel and stay in good hotels are getting ideas about bedroom design from those experiences. And the versatility of a highly comfortable but flexible space is one aspect that modern luxury hotels have contributed to people's expectations of bedrooms.

After the master bedroom has been fitted out, whether lavishly or in spare comfort, thoughts turn to children's rooms and guest bedrooms. 'And mighty proud I am ... that I am able to have a spare bed for my friends,' said the seventeenth-century English diarist Samuel Pepys. It is a great pleasure to be able to offer a guest a bed, even better a room of their own. In a guest room there might be more consideration given to general comfort, a bed that is well dressed, some easy storage and perhaps a little desk area. Guest rooms are good places to make use of quirky furnishings, such as a vintage desk or dresser, which you adore but doesn't suit the master suite. A chest of drawers that was irresistible at the brocanteur, a rug that has travelled with you from student days, a cherished little lamp that belonged to a grandmother, these are objects that offer a personal welcome from you to overnight guests.

Of all the rooms in the house, children's bedrooms are the most fun to design and decorate. Perhaps it is because in planning our children's bedrooms we are allowed to immerse ourselves in our own childhood memories and conjure our most beloved games, stories, toys, fantasies and that inimitable sense of wonder. In this chapter we show not the over-indulged bedrooms of celebrity extravagance but rooms that use colour and shape in playful combinations to create bright areas for sleeping, playing, doing homework and daydreaming. Most of these are simpler arrangements than we often see for designer children's spaces, but they are all delightfully inviting. A fairytale-style canopy bed in an old farmhouse, a small, wonderfully secretive painted sleeping alcove, a four-poster covered in patterns of pink, a modern set of built-in bunk beds, these are the range of options for sleeping that make us all wish we could be children again, at least for a day or a night.

It is the sense of fun that we allow ourselves when decorating for children that we shouldn't lose hold of in the rest of our design decisions. A house that isn't afraid to be fun is not afraid to be welcoming. And welcome brings the peace that we need for rest. Children might, after they check under the bed for monsters, go to sleep dreaming of flying away with Peter Pan, a guest might feel grateful for a comfortable mattress and a soft pillow. We might all have different ideas of what kind of room we most like to sleep in and what kind of bed feels best, but everyone feels better after a good night's slumber.

The artistic impulse means that all the rooms are infused with creative energy. Even sleeping areas are rich with inspiration.

Below The large bedroom of a Parisian apartment includes a sunken platform bath and is covered with an assortment of kilim rugs. The vintage chairs provide a retro spirit.

Above A bold mix of geometric patterns makes a lively atmosphere in a painter's Parisian loft.

Right The rustic atmosphere of this modern Nordic country house is emphasized by natural log columns and cow-skin bedding.

Retro style combines a healthy nostalgia with good design sense, and the knowledge that classic furnishings never go out of style.

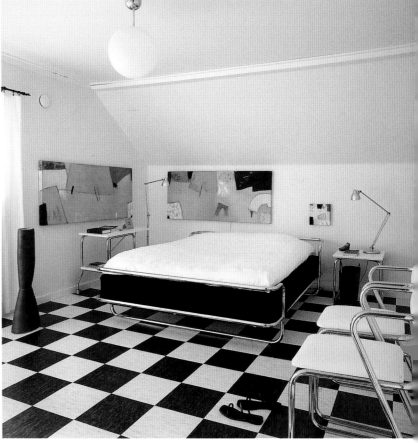

Above left A combined bedroom and bath space on the mezzanine floor of a Marseilles conversion features a classic 'Butterfly' chair.

Left In an attic bedroom, the leather bedstead is complemented by an old leather Louis Vuitton trunk used as a wardrobe.

Above The steel-framed bed and chairs and the black-and-white-patterned floor define this Art Deco-style bedroom.

Opposite In a South African villa, a feeling of utter luxury is achieved in a bedroom that opens fully to the outdoor terrace.

In his apartment in Ibiza interior designer Victor Esposito has retained elements of traditional style with open beams and patterned tiles throughout. The cabinet and translucent 'Tulip' chair, through the doorway, establish a retro style.

An old advertisement printed on cloth is used as a colourful backdrop for a simple bed arrangement. Eames chairs and a small table form a seating area.

Masculine rooms achieve elegance by simple arrangements. But even these can have a flourish or two.

Opposite The neat wooden cupboards against white walls make a sharp contrast in a restored house in Provence. The white bed hangings add a bit of softness.

Right A bedroom in the roof space is kept from feeling cramped with simple furnishings and a natural wooden floor. White walls are warmed up with some neutral fabrics.

Below Enclosed with a tassled theatre curtain, this bed is set for drama.

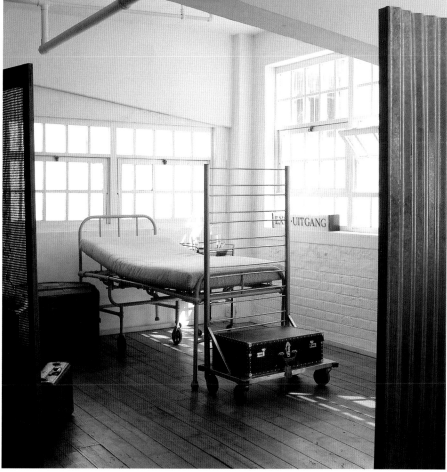

Right A South African loft features a mechanical hospital bed. Partitions separate the space from the open area.

Antique furnishings and objects add a pleasant sense of history and charm to any room, but in the bedroom they have a particular allure.

Above Support for bed curtains is created in a modern fashion – not by posters or a canopy but by suspending a metal framework from the ceiling.

Above right A four-poster canopy bed with an imposing carved headboard commands the master bedroom of a traditional-style villa in Majorca.

Opposite below A simple Swedish bedroom bears the hallmark pale-coloured furnishings and ceramic-tiled fireplace.

Right This house in the South of France has been restored with the original décor, including painted ceiling beams, plasterwork and a sleeping alcove.

Decorative effects on walls and surfaces turn a bedroom into a little jewel box of art.

Right Patterns and colour brighten a small room with a carved sleigh bed.

Below Distempered colour on the walls and ethnic coverings give this room an exotic ambience.

Above The red fabric lampshade and deep tone of the walls, together with the open fire, make this room a pocket of warmth.

Left An alcove bed dominates a small Nordic bedroom. Natural wood and flooring contribute to the clean, rustic simplicity.

Below The house of designer Karel Fonteyne in Menorca is full of colourful displays. The mustard yellow and the blue have a particularly North African feel. The chandelier and patterned floor feel much more European.

Animal patterns in the bedroom, real or faux, have an exuberant, playful appeal.

A bed under the eaves conjures visions of fairytales and secret hideaways, even for adults.

Above This top-level bedroom in a converted stable enjoys an airy space under the beams.

Above right In the attic bedroom of a South African farmhouse the roof thatch is part of the interior décor.

Right Stone and painted board meet in the slanting roof space of a Swedish island home.

Opposite Artist Yuri Kuper transformed a Normandy barn into a spacious house and studio. The ancient A-frame construction is apparent in the top-floor bedroom.

Opposite Enchanting sleeping spaces in the eaves are made more appealing with timber construction and soft natural light. These small spaces make paring down essential but each object takes on a special charm.

This page A bedroom can be for much more than sleeping, here a good selection of books and a desk space are an added bonus.

Built-in beds

have a particular
charm, being both
wonderfully compact
and satisfyingly
bespoke.

Romantic rooms are those that combine comfort with sensuous details such as soft hangings, intimate lighting and a few objects of particular beauty.

Canopies and bed curtains have real imaginative appeal, the suggestion of exotic adventure and romance. Even a bit of draped netting transforms a bed from mundane to enticing.

Below A bed draped in crowned netting is a little haven in a high-ceilinged space.

Opposite The striped hangings on this four-poster in Morocco are part of a world of pattern with the mosaics, the tile floor and the coloured-diamond rug.

Above Patterned textiles and cloudy white hangings make this high-ceilinged room in Provence seem magical rather than cramped.

Ethnic elements come to the fore when combined with chic European minimalism: the tactile sensations of clay tiles and bare plaster are highlighted by fine modern styling.

Above Built-in elements like this wall niche with the jewel-box window and arched opening signify the North African style.

Left The simplicity of the plaster walls and floors is emphasized by the decorative wooden door.

Opposite With its neutral tones and spare wall decoration, this large bedroom in Provence has a light and airy feel.

Bare concrete is often thought of as a wholly modern material, but its elemental appeal has ancient associatio

that reach out to other periods and cultures.

Right and below Charming single beds under the eaves make a perfectly cosy offering for guests, especially with bright bed curtains.

Right An antique lamp with a decorative shade picks up the floral motif of a scenic wallcovering. The finely worked table cloth and crisp bed linen balance the exuberant pattern.

Guest rooms are good places to indulge in more whimsical sleeping arrangements, while still creating little havens of comfort.

Above A guest room does not usually include bunk beds, but they are perfect for overnight visitors, especially younger ones.

Above right This intimate space in the eaves makes a compact, but enchanting spare bedroom.

Right In the old days beds were stacked anywhere they could fit. This cottage in Norway makes good use of an awkward juncture under the eaves.

Children's rooms give us leave to express a sense of fun and whimsy, and also a bit of nostalgia.

Opposite The curtained bed is like its own playhouse, while the stencilled floor pattern is playful but not overtly childish.

Above An efficient use of space with the bed set on top of storage under the eaves also makes an intriguing play area.

Above right What child wouldn't love a bed tucked into an alcove? Keeping the furnishings simple leaves more space for play.

Right Another bed under the eaves demonstrates how the small space can be transformed for older children or adults.

Below Children's spaces don't have to be all primary colours or soft pastels. Neutrals work also, leaving space for a bright imagination.

Above The driftwood shelf has a fairytale quality, perfect for displaying found objects.

Right A light fitting that resembles a bunch of balloons is just the thing for a little pink retreat.

Below left A more mature room with a zebra-patterned rug and dark, four-poster bed.

Below right This four-poster bed has a more grown-up feeling, while brightly patterned blankets and throws add an element of fun.

Above left Patchwork and striped ticking fabric, an old school desk and reclaimed wooden doors create an old-fashioned feel.

Left A child's room in a Dutch home mixes modern materials, such as the steel-framed bed, with a traditional quilt and furnishings.

Above A newly built modern chalet features custom-made bunk beds in pale wood; they are both elegant and practical.

Opposite Natural light pours into a child's room from a pair of corner windows, making a perfect place for doing homework or daydreaming.

A basin and counter carved by the sculptor J. B. Blunk for his Californian house has a finely ridged detail. Its visible grain and texture are a celebration of the material.

BATHROOM

The bathroom has evolved enormously just in the last century. As anyone who has ever lived in an older house will know, the attitude and amount of care and attention paid to this room in the past are nothing like what we are willing, or find necessary, to set aside in terms of space, and budget, today. When converting an older property, even if just fifty years old, the most necessary improvements are usually carried out in the kitchen and the bathroom. This is obviously to do with advances in appliances and technology, but also a matter of taste. No longer considered just a functional room, the bathroom offers a whole experience of bathing, showering and some amount of pampering.

The most significant recent innovation is in the mechanical systems of bathrooms, not just the moving indoors of the plumbing and having hot water on tap, but in the gadgetry that now goes along with our daily ablutions. In a little more than a century in many places households have gone from having to go outside to use a WC and heating water on a stove-top for a bath, to demanding heated flooring and towel rails and showers enclosed in seamless glass. Now there is even high-tech glass that can be made to turn opaque with the flick of a switch and the ignition of a small electrical current. This means that in some very modern houses the bathroom walls can be totally transparent until someone steps inside. It all goes to show that in most

Above Adding a bit of classical refinement to a period-style bathroom, a goddess figurine holds a pile of towels. The 'Ghost' chair by Philippe Starck is an edgy modern element.

Left Luxury is in the details, a vintage table, a pitcher and a bottle of scented oil.

Opposite In a modern American summer house, with typical white-painted timber panels, the raised bath presents a view of the sea.

houses today bathing is something that is not only effortless, but also in some cases quietly indulgent, not just a matter of practical hygiene but rituals to be celebrated.

Yet, we are not so very unusual in our desire to have clean bodies and to enjoy ourselves while bathing. The Ancient Romans loved baths. They built large complexes devoted to bathing, which entailed communal, social activities. A typical bathing house would usually have cold, warm and hot baths, as well as an exercise area and a swimming pool. And during the Middle Ages in northern Europe people were more concerned with cleanliness than we give them credit for. Even in England bathing was more common then than is popularly believed. Bath houses for both genders were popular until the spread of disease gave them a bad name and convinced lawmakers to close them down. Then it wasn't until the nineteenth century when steady water supplies and adequate sewerage systems were introduced, that bathing could become a regular practice for most people.

Nowadays we see bathing as not only a necessity but also something to be enhanced by new developments in technology and extensive use of wonderfully perfumed products. In this chapter we have bathrooms that meet all of the requirements of being both useful and inspiring. Some are rustic in style, but beautifully crafted, while others are gleaming with modern materials, and some marry a twenty-first-century environment with old-fashioned fixtures, and vice versa.

Many of the rooms in this chapter demonstrate how trends might be taken up but then adapted to a particular setting. Open shower 'rooms' have been around for decades in warmer climates but have become popular in European homes only fairly recently. This is akin to having an open-plan interior in the bathroom. Gone are partitioned little cubicles, except perhaps for a separate WC, as the development of better waterproofing methods has meant that the entire bathing space can be left undivided without having to worry about leaks anywhere in the floor. The materials then, like a beautiful deep-hued slate tile, can be

carried through all around the room, making a modernist haven.

The open room is part of a growing popularity of 'spa-style' bathrooms in private homes. A bath or shower that features water jets at the sides and settings for different types of spray are among the amenities that are available to make bathing more of a luxury experience. There are some who have gone so far as to add their own sauna, in its own separate room, but as part of their main bathing area.

Some people who have rethought the bathroom concept and found standard models uninspiring have opted to break out of the enclosed space altogether. They might choose to put a free-standing tub in the middle of the bedroom, instead of inserting a rectangular vessel into a corner of the bathroom. This makes a particularly romantic set-up especially if there happens to be an open fire nearby, and puts the tub more on show. An old, deep, claw-footed bath reminds us of just how precious a full hot soak once was. Now it becomes the focus of a large bathroom design scheme and inspires further decorative flourishes like some classical statuary or even a crystal chandelier. One indulgent example features a pooling length of fabric suspended above the bath, more an extravagance of drapery than a practical shower curtain.

Modern tubs tend to be much simpler, with some designers trying to create the purest form in a single material without any seams or joints. Materials have changed with baths too. From the old cast-iron tubs that are wonderful pieces of nostalgia, but tend to cool down quickly, to the modern versions that are simple to keep and care for, there are also some interesting variations in between. Here we have wooden bathtubs, some well-crafted rectangular forms and one rounded and banded in metal like an elongated cask. Basins too appear in a greater variety of materials than we normally see in the pages of popular home catalogues. There are carved wooden basins, conical stone and metallic basins that rise up from the floor, double basins in modern composite materials and old-fashioned pedestal sinks that offer more space and establish a distinctively old world atmosphere.

In recent decades the fully coordinated, built-in bathroom has become de rigeur, but here we see that there is no impediment to making your own arrangement with an antique chest, a vintage armchair, a decorative framed mirror and other personal choices that demonstrate that it is the resident and not a builder or developer (or even an architect) who has kitted out this particular space. Furniture can be chosen as easily as a paint colour or a tile pattern. And even tiles offer a surprisingly generous variety of choice. Clean granite, wonderfully textured riven slate, vintage ceramics and unique mosaic designs fill the pages that follow, further testament to the fact that the bathroom can be one of the most creative rooms in the house.

And while we reconsider the closed-off nature of the bathroom, with the idea of open shower rooms, we can also appreciate the luxuriant effect of a room that is open to lots of natural light. Although a long soak with the lights dimmed and the perfume of scented candles is an absolute joy, perhaps no other room in the house benefits as much from natural light. Some of the more innovative designs are those that could be termed 'back to nature' in their use of skylights, large windows and, in one instance, an entire corner wall around the shower open to the forest outside. Taking this a step further, in fact, there are some designs that are located outside, a shower against a bold mosaic patterned wall outside a house in South Africa, a timber outdoor shower in Norway, a culture determined to make the most of outdoor living whatever the weather.

All in all, what the spaces on the following pages demonstrate in vivid detail is that every room in the house is open to change and interpretation, that accepted models of luxury and taste do not need to take precedence over personal style and that function often benefits from a bit of fun and an eye for beauty.

A picture of contemporary comfort, a dark granite tub enclosure in a room filled with light from a charming paned double window. The day-bed offers a relaxing place to sit in the sun after a warm bath.

Left A modern bathroom in a South African house includes a mix of materials: wooden cupboards, slate tiles around the bath and stainless-steel twin basins.

Below left Made from Lebanese cedar, this Japanese-inspired bath sits in soft light created by a backlit wall beyond.

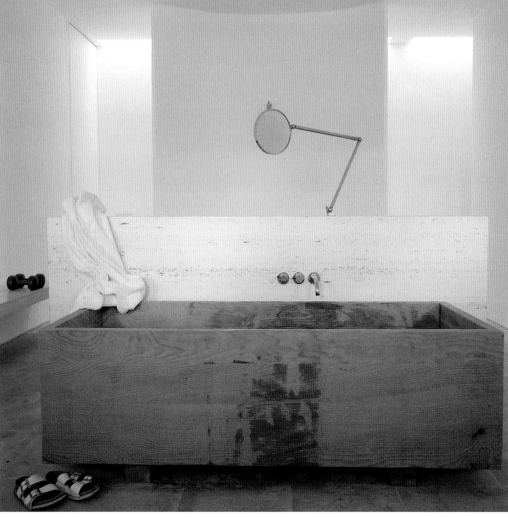

Above The bathroom in a Parisian apartment is all cool modern geometry but in soft neutral tones.

Opposite Stone is the predominant material in this Mallorcan bathroom with small punctured window openings. The dividing shelf and basin are carved from local Santanyi stone.

Stone is one of the most elemental materials. The variety in texture, colour and pattern is infinite, but the feeling of natural stone always has a fundamental appeal.

Opposite The bath in the guest quarters of this converted farm outbuilding is an essay in contrast. The room with its old stone walls and worn timber beams has been enhanced with polished concrete, a modern conical basin and some touches of luxury such as the decorative mirror and candlesticks.

Above In Ireland, the claw-footed bath and antique mirrored cabinet bring a bit of period style to the rustic backdrop of bared brick and stripped pine.

Above right A modern house in Ibiza has been carefully designed to allow the stone cliff to intrude and become part of the interior.

Right This bathing area in a South African safari camp has plenty of rugged ambience and features a metal screen and wash basin created by a local artist.

Above This sauna-style bathing space has been fully lined in timber slats, which can weather the wet and dry conditions beautifully.

Below A modern bathroom clad in dark wood features a separate sauna room.

Opposite A cottage in the Estonian forest has a clean-lined but gently rustic atmosphere. The oval bath is made of timber banded with metal, similar to the construction of a wine cask.

Wood has an instinctive allure, even in bathing spaces, with its rich natural tones and textures and its natural durability.

Below The roof and walls of designer Pedro Espirito's Portuguese beach cottage are traditional thatch, which he has left uncovered on the interior.

Above The rough timber plank walls and stone floor of this rustic Nordic retreat have been tamed with a few modern accessories.

Opposite The Scandinavian summer house of architect Hans Parr Lampe preserves its rustic, old-fashioned charm.

Industrial chic has even made it into the modern bathing experience. The combination of raw metals and overtly functional details with softer elements creates a new modern look.

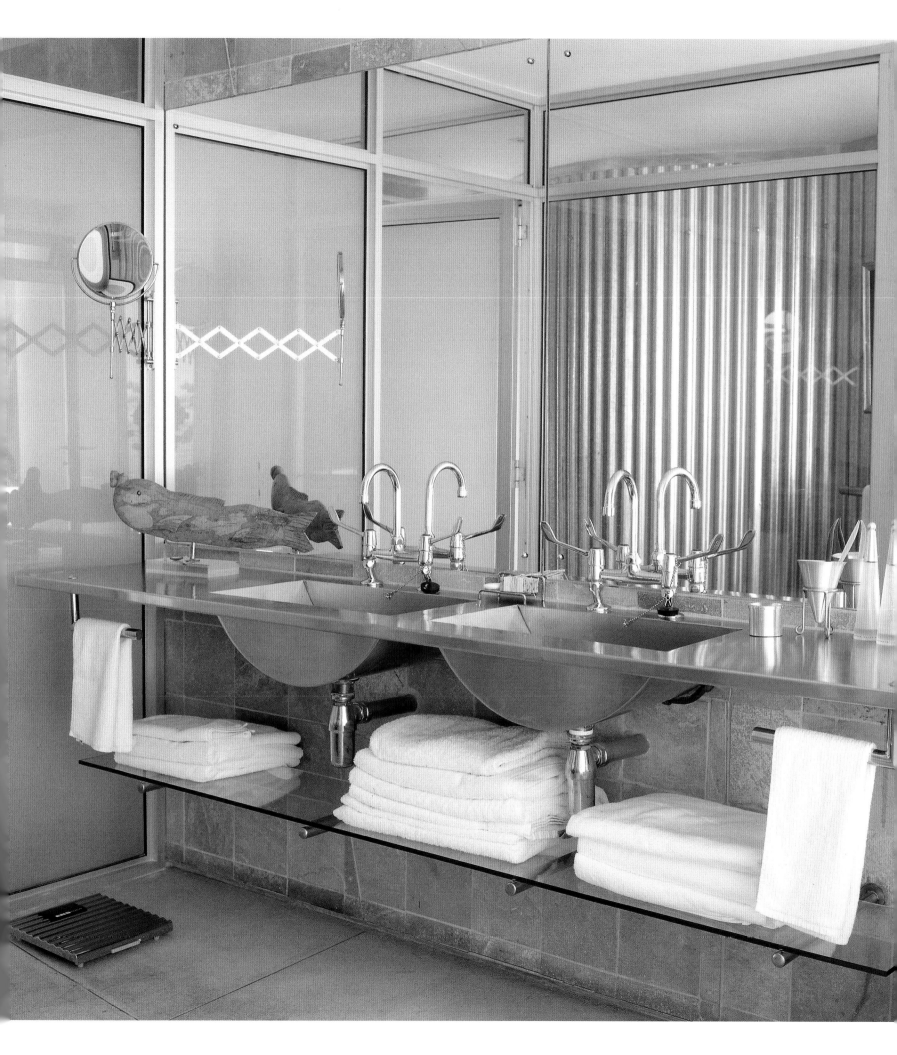

Period details are not just the preserve of living spaces, and they are appealing as part of an eclectic interior scheme.

Opposite above A wooden folding screen covered in embroidered linen, a claw-footed bath and wrought-iron storage basket evoke the atmosphere of a previous time. The pale wall colour has a more modern feel.

Opposite below, left and right Only the patterned floor tiles suggest the Spanish heritage of this space. The aqua wall tiles and pedestal basin introduce a touch of Art Deco style.

Right The owners of this townhouse in the South of France have chosen to preserve some of the best period details, such as the claw-footed bath, the terracotta floor tiles and the marble-topped basin and cupboard.

Above Pretty patterned floor tiles add colour and warmth to a white-themed bathroom in Norway.

Right A spacious bathing area in the restored Greek Revival house of American antiques dealer Richard Kazarian. The white-painted wood and white walls make a clean backdrop for pieces from his personal collection.

Left The large bathing area of a grand, Italian-inspired villa features a freestanding bath with turn-of-the-century-style taps. White marble floor tiles lead to a balcony beyond.

Below Soft, subdued light filters through windows in the pitched roof of this attic bathroom in England.

Above Antique and modern meet
again in this crisply designed
bathroom with cast-iron tub
and carved wooden chair used
as a bathside table.

Opposite The details of this historic house in Norway are all on display: the old-fashioned ceramic wood-burning stove, the classical moulding, the pedestal basin, the framed mirror and the ceiling light.

Above What better way to relax than in a big old-fashioned bath set beneath a crystal chandelier?

Above right This tiny bathing space in a cottage in Maine is still full of style.

Right Ogden Codman, Jr co-wrote the famous nineteenth-century style bible, *The Decoration of Houses*, with the American author Edith Wharton. Here in the Federal Revival house he designed in the fashionable resort area of Newport, Rhode Island, his fondness for a kind of embellished classicism is in evidence.

Above left Retro is made new with a vibrant wall colour and artwork by the owner.

Above The addition of antique wooden doors, terracotta tiles around the bath and an ethnic rug turn this bathroom into a little pocket of culture.

Left The diamond-patterned tile around the bath and the terracotta floor tiles signal the design heritage of this Provençal house.

Opposite The light, airy bathing space shows the former character of this converted stables. The ball-foot tub and freestanding shower emphasize a luxury of space and light.

Decorative effects can reinvigorate a space. A small bathroom with vivid colour and pattern becomes a bright haven of relaxation.

Left The bold mosaic on the shower wall of this South African house is a work of art.

Above Taking the cool blue of the Mediterranean as his cue, the owner of this bathroom in Menorca also painted the partition wall to bring in the colour of golden sun. The basin is piedra de mares sandstone.

Opposite Not everything is as it seems in this Provençal house. The walls have been painted to resemble large tiles and the bath painted to match. The shower curtain in draped linen swaps functional for romantic.

This page A room combines the modern aspect of coloured mosaic tiles with another period flavour in the form of a large oval mirror in an ornate, carved gilt frame.

Opposite Pebbles from the Durance river in France have been set in rough concrete to create a delicate frieze and mirror-frame effect.

Hammam is a word for a Turkish bath that implies not just bathing but a whole ritual of heat, steam, massage and cooling, a therapeutic process of relaxation.

Opposite The wall and rug have complementary geometric patterns in this Spanish bathing space. A filigree lantern on a traditional stool reflects the local Moorish heritage.

Above A water trough for animals has been brought indoors. A few tiles purchased from a Barcelona flea market provide plenty of decorative pattern and colour.

Right An old stone basin is redolent with age and integrity. The swirls of the wrought-iron chair make a stunning contrast.

The concrete bath is much more luxurious than the name suggests. The continuous use of a material such as polished concrete imposes a sense of glamour but also a comfortable, elemental quality.

Shower rooms have evolved from pocket-sized cupboards to lavish open spaces full of light.

This page A clever use of curves gives this open shower the illusion of an outdoor space.

Opposite The glass-cornered shower is open to a forest view, with the natural vegetation screening the user from prying eyes.

Opposite The freedom of outdoor showering is enhanced by the beauty of a bold mosaic wall mural.

Above Sauna-style timber partitions frame this outdoor shower.

Above right A driftwood sculpture becomes an outdoor shower and towel rail in Corsica.

Right White-washed exterior walls make a partial enclosure aided by natural shelter offered by trees and shrubs in Ibiza.

TEXTURE

Style projected through a love of texture gives us a real connection to place and materials.

We naturally respond to patterns
in nature and to those we create.
Pattern suggests order (when not
overdone) and can be used to
great effect when a fine balance
is achieved.

ACKNOWLEDGMENTS

Over the years, I have had the privilege of travelling extensively and meeting some very special and creative people in many different countries. They invited me into their private sphere, into their homes, and allowed me to document them.

I am hugely grateful to each one of these homeowners.

SOURCES

Judith Flanders, 'The Victorian House', *The Spectator*, 2003

Witold Rybczynski, *Home: A Short History of an Idea*, London, 1988

Peter Thornton, *Authentic Decor: The Domestic Interior, 1620–1920*, London, 2000

First published in the United Kingdom in 2013 by Thames & Hudson Ltd, 181A High Holborn, London WC1V 7QX

Real Homes © 2013 Thames & Hudson Ltd, London
Photographs © 2013 Solvi dos Santos

All Rights Reserved. No part of this publication may be reproduced or transmitted in any form or by any means, electronic or mechanical, including photocopy, recording or any other information storage and retrieval system, without prior permission in writing from the publisher.

British Library Cataloguing-in-Publication Data

A catalogue record for this book is available from the British Library

ISBN 978-0-500-51686-7

Manufactured in China by Imago

To find out about all our publications, please visit **www.thamesandhudson.com**. There you can subscribe to our e-newsletter, browse or download our current catalogue, and buy any titles that are in print.